MEDIAEVAL FLOOR TILES

By the same author
BRICK BUILDING IN ENGLAND

ii

Mediaeval Floor Tiles

Jane A Wight

St. Martin's Press New York

All rights reserved. For information, write:
St. Martin's Press, Inc., 175 Fifth Avenue,
New York, N.Y. 10010
Printed in Great Britain
Library of Congress Catalog Card Number: 75-18592
First published in the United States of America in 1975

Contents

Illustrations

FIGURES

Notes on the author's drawings

Mosaic Where black is used in the illustrations of mosaic tiling it represents the darker of two colours, or the darkest of three colours.

Figured tiles Unless it is specified in the captions that they are relief tiles, and so of one colour only, all the figured tiles illustrated are two-colour inlaid or printed tiles. If black is used it represents the glazed earthenware ground, but it may normally be assumed that subjects or motifs were done in the pale clay. Most of the square tiles shown without surface measurements are between $4\frac{1}{2}$ and $5\frac{1}{2}$ inches square, but the Wessex and Malvern-style tiles were made rather larger.

Tiles with abstract or geometrical designs are very much more common than the selection of illustrations suggests, but the number and range of different geometrical designs is proportionately smaller.

All figures are drawn by the author with the exception of figure 8, which is reproduced by kind permission of The Guildhall Library, City of London, and the repeating pattern in figure 42, which was drawn by Julia Ball, after a tracing by Dr A. B. Emden.

Acknowledgements

I am very grateful for the massive, unrewarded aid given by so many people to this study of decorated tiles. Their disinterested kindness has benefited the publishers too, though I gladly record here my gratitude for the welcoming interest and courtesy of Mr J D Newth and Louisa Browne. I suspect that some of the kind people who provided information did so so long ago that they have forgotten, because the demands of *Brick Building in England from the Middle Ages to 1550* have intervened. The full list of acknowledgements would be unmanageably long, so I can only apologise for all the omissions and mention just the main or multiple contributors. Among the people not named are patient librarians, museum staff, clergymen and the custodians of old buildings.

Exemplary help has come from the City Librarian of Bristol, the Reference Librarians at Aylesbury and Chertsey, Miss D. J. Philipps and the reference library staff at Reading, and from the Essex County Archivist.

My main debts are to *Hallam Ashley*, for photographs; the *Rev. G. Armstrong* of Ashbourne, Derbyshire; *Julia Ball*, my cousin, for hospitality and the Broughton tile repeat; *Teresa Barling* (now Thomas), who took me a very long time ago to Haccombe Chapel in Devon, where the tiles converted me to this interest; *Mr Andrew Borthwick* of Chipstead Tiles (London), for Victorian information; *Miss J. Burnett Brown* of Lacock Abbey, Wiltshire; *Diana Bullock*, for tracings of the Clifton House tiles (used with the permission of King's Lynn Borough Council); *Mr R C Burnett*, Custodian of Byland Abbey; the *Rev. G. Burningham* of Morley, Derbyshire; *Dr Francis Celoria* of Keele University, for illustrations of Victorian machinery; *Mr B. C. Doughty,* Clerk of Works (acting for the Dean and Chapter of Canterbury Cathedral), for tracings and rubbings; *K. M. Dowdall*; *Mrs E. S. Eames*, for oral information, supplementing her vital articles and *Handbook*; *Mary Ann Ebert*, Redditch; *Dr A. B. Emden*, for information and for the Broughton and Sherborne tile designs; the *Rev. J. W. Evans*, for information about tiles at St. David's and Carew, Pembrokeshire. *Mr Alan V. Franklin,* Senior Verger at Ely Cathedral; all the *Gotches*, for hospitality, transport

x

and other help, especially at Chastleton; *Mr J. Patrick Greene,* Field Archaeologist, Runcorn Development Corporation; *Mrs L. Hamand,* for much help over the Malvern tiles, besides a copy of James Nott's *History* of Malvern Priory; *Mr Michael Hamand* for the colour photographs of Malvern tiles and permission to use them; *Martin Horne; Mary Lloyd,* for transport to places in Gloucestershire, Herefordshire, Worcestershire and Shropshire; *Mary Power,* whose help included a saving Latin reference to Psalm 26; *Stan* and *Bernie Robertson,* for transport and photographs in Essex, Hertfordshire and Berkshire; *Sheila* and *Alan Slavin;* the *Rev. T. H. W. Swann* of Sawtry, Huntingdonshire; *Mr E. Tompkins,* Custodian of Cleeve Abbey; *Ruthanne Tudball,* for tracings and editing. *Miss Norma R. Whitcomb* has most generously let me use some heraldic designs and the three patterns from Bradgate House from her catalogue of 260 Leicestershire tile designs (1956). I am especially grateful to those people who took tracings, rubbings or measurements for me—and cheerfully failed to complain about the chill climates they therefore experienced.

For vital information and help over the Southam (Gloucestershire) tiles, a late 'discovery' for me, I must specially thank *Allan Ledger, Mary Lloyd, Mrs D. Winkless* and *Mr and Mrs M. Cannon.*

CHAPTER ONE

Subject, design and survival

This study is intended just as an introduction to a promising but neglected subject. It is mainly for amateurs, and rests on the belief that our immediate and visual responses are valuable. There is still plenty of room for thought about these designs, both the ordinary and the exceptional, and the subject of mediaeval decorated tiles has been popularly neglected, while nearly all the scholarly work on it is hidden away in journals. Remarkably, this is the first book on mediaeval English tiles to be published since 1858. It is necessary that interest in the subject should grow, since the tiles themselves are often not cared for. Even in so deliberately guarded a place as St. Albans Abbey, I have seen heavy concrete slabs lodged edgewise (at the best angle for chipping the surface) on some of the few remaining tiles, ones in good condition and certainly interesting. These pavings should be sought out and protected in their original locations, not just in the cases of a museum. It is hoped through this book to make people aware of the virtues of looking downwards as well as upwards in churches, where floor tiles and roof bosses and glass can bear similar motifs, or where coloured tiles may be pictured at the feet of painted saints on the wooden chancel screen or of glass saints and donors in the windows.

Our tiles are survivors out of a total population of unknown extent, all at risk since the Middle Ages. Improved post-mediaeval views on comfort banished them from houses, though less often from churches. At least from the Puritan Commonwealth onwards, however, figured tiles were also liable to be removed from churches – in favour of plain replacements of tile or stone – either for religious reasons or for mere tidiness.

Since no sustained attempt will be made to enter the minds of the original creators and viewers of tiles, a perhaps anachronistic opening idea may be permitted to us: to place patiently shaped or decorated objects to be trampled on the floor suggests a gracious prodigality in the people who paid for them. That we can still benefit in many buildings from the largesse of this seemingly impractical ornamentation proves the technical skill of many makers. Often only the bright glazes have been trodden away. White clay inlays have survived the disappearance of the glaze, that gave them – and the setting – richer colouring, so that the patterns at least are known. In ruined Yorkshire monasteries twelfth- or thirteenth-century mosaic floors of dark and light tiles have survived the Dissolution by nearly four-and-a-half centuries, though the glossy surfaces may have been worn away.

Tiles are an area of muted mediaevalism well worth looking into. The antiquarian concentration of interest has been on the exceptional, the high quality tiles such as those of 'Wessex' and Malvern, the superb and protected floor of Westminster Abbey's octagonal Chapter House and on tiles or tile fragments with literary or legendary references.

These 'literary' tiles are pictorial or illustrative, needing elaborate explanation of their motifs. Examples are the Tristram and Isolde series from Chertsey; the eccentric 'sgraffito', that is scratched or drawn, tiles from Tring that tell the violent Apocryphal story of Christ's Infancy; tiles with difficult and abbreviated inscriptions in Black Letter; and the Westminster Abbey Chapter House design of Edward the Confessor giving his ring to a beggar. The point is that the pictorial tiles, if of any complexity, do what was more appropriate to manuscript illustration or to mural paintings. Not only may they need a text, but they are not primarily tile designs, with the design specifically fitted to the usual square shape of the tile.

It should be admitted that the distinction between pictorial and non-pictorial is not easily made. Beautiful work may succeed as ornament even if the legends shown are unknown to the viewer. It may seem artificial, for instance, to label a tiny part of the Westminster Abbey pavement as literary and the rest non-literary, but it has been suggested that those few tiles with human figures were intruders from a Westminster Palace floor. One complication is that

2

tile designs might begin in a limited way and end in wider use for their decorative quality. This is well demonstrated by a group of inlaid tiles excavated at Reading Abbey which carry a spiky, abstract-looking pattern: their tile stamp was earlier designed to form the lower half of a robed figure, certainly an ecclesiastic. The upper half has nowhere survived. At Reading, numbers of the lower half – with pointed shoes, heavy drapery and long sleeve ends – were used in a mass, some set diagonally, obviously just for decoration. The same movement from the specific to the general is shown by the common and attractive tiles inlaid with the boast of family heraldy: these tiles, with their geometrical charges, rampant lions and curvaceous pigs, were first meant for churches where the bearers were patrons but soon reached mass distribution.

The general point remains, that the historians have displayed most interest in relatively complex figured tiles. The archaeologists, perhaps naturally, have been more interested in identifying tiles than in judging or publicising them. Little attention, apart from in the now very rare Victorian tomes – thickly illustrated with woodcuts or engravings – has been paid to plain mosaic tiles, the oldest type. With the exception of the famous and *unusual* examples from Chertsey, the transitional style of mosaic inlaid with further patterns has also been largely ignored or underestimated: this may have been as a consequence of the tidy categorisation of tiles by their method of manufacture. Even the most common later mediaeval figured tiles – the ones we are most likely to find *in situ* today – have been undervalued. Indeed, one has encountered expert opinion attacking the quality of these ordinary, pleasant tiles with the kind of indignation which used to be reserved for flights of plaster ducks.

Inlaid mosaic tiles are very often especially interesting: they are of various shapes, carrying simple inlaid designs, and are used either as minor elements in two- or three-colour mosaic or – the examples are rarer, but Redditch parish church (Worcestershire) has some – in wholly inlaid floors. The general trend was away from plain mosaic, made in the Cistercian monasteries and difficult to bake satisfactorily, to the wide use of the easier and more practical square figured tiles – these predominantly with slip designs.

There may have been more inlaid mosaic than is apparent now, but pavements of this bridging type must have been especially vulnerable to wear and replacement. In a strict or pedantic sense

3

mosaic was unnecessary with inlaid work, which could form external as well as internal patterning – making circles, quatrefoils and other shapes across the edges of the squares. Among the square tiles we even find textile-style designs of simplified foliage, which can run on in any direction. There is a particularly ingenious 'incomplete' design like this in the prior's chapel at Castle Acre (Norfolk), with thin upright stems punctuated by pairs of irregular trefoil leaves. Such patterns were successors to those favoured rectangular border tiles that formed rows of inlaid foliage scrolls, but they were more adaptable and so better suited to a mass market.

There has been a lack of interest in design for its own sake, though there have been various illustrated studies of regional patterns, such as those of Penn (Buckinghamshire) or the embossed tiles of Warwickshire. Some of the ordinary tiles *are* relatively cheap and nasty, but others were carefully planned, relating content to the usual square of four-and-a-half, five or six inches. Knights on horseback were a favoured mediaeval design but often a clumsy one. Often, in fact, these figures are far less effective than the simple and most popular motif of all, the fleur-de-lis of the Virgin Mary, who was regarded as the best intercessor with God. Tiles carrying human figures are not common, partly because they were not used for the repeating patterns that made up the bulk of a floor, and probably partly also because their fussier and more irregular lines have been more prone to wear. Such designs were often comparatively crude and, if any detail was wanted, cramped. When they are found in fragments only it is most frustrating to try to reconstruct their original designs. It is perhaps significant that in the Great Malvern revival of fine inlays, in the mid-fifteenth century, the human figure as well as the horse is ignored in favour of religious emblems, heraldry and foliage.

There are hundreds of fleur-de-lis designs, from the early fine and fernlike inlays of the Wessex tiles to the more thickset Penn types of the fourteenth century. To amass examples of this one motif, usually set diagonally on the tile, is as intriguing in its way as docketing the fine details of Westminster's Chertsey tiles that include scaly pugnacious pikes; curling dragons; griffins; enthroned king and queen; and musicians. The very quantity of the fleur-de-lis patterns suggests that restless perfectionism was more common than the copying of other people's old or worn-out stamps. The fitting of content to frame

4

a, b, c

d, e, f

g, h, i

1   FLEUR-DE-LIS DESIGNS (*not to scale*)
(a) C 14 Wessex tile from Romsey Abbey, Hampshire, one of set of four forming repeated fleurs-de-lis (British Museum).
(b) C 14 tile at Rievaulx Abbey, Yorkshire, also an inlaid quadrant tile.
(c) C 14 heraldic tile probably made at Nottingham (British Museum).
(d) Tile of about 1255, with foliate fleur-de-lis, in Westminster Abbey Chapter House.
(e) C 14 tile from Bordesley Abbey (Tardebrigge), in St. Stephen's Church, Redditch, Worcestershire.
(f) Fleur-de-lis with flower-like stamens, from C 14 tiles at Dilwyn Church, Herefordshire. (Some foliage at edges of tile is worn.)
(g) C 14 tile at Clifton House, King's Lynn, Norfolk.
(h) Later mediaeval tile in St. Albans Abbey, Hertfordshire.
(i) C 14 tile at Rievaulx Abbey, Yorkshire.

5

a, b, c

d, e, f

g, h, i

2   FLEUR-DE-LIS DESIGNS (*not to scale*)

(a) Later mediaeval tile at Edelsborough Church, Buckinghamshire.

(b) C 14 relief tile from Bawsey, Norfolk (example in British Museum).

(c) Later mediaeval tile in Cookham-on-Thames Church, Berkshire, probably made at Burnham in Buckinghamshire.

(d) Later mediaeval Penn-type tile: this is a very common pattern found, for example at Blewbury, Padworth and West Hendred churches in Berkshire. The quadrants form circles and quatrefoils.

(e) Later mediaeval tile at Sutton Courtenay Church, Berkshire.

(f) Later mediaeval tile at Sandridge Church, Hertfordshire.

(g) (h) (i) C 14 inlaid tiles at Rievaulx Abbey, Yorkshire.

a, b, c

d, e, f

g, h, i

3   FLEUR-DE-LIS DESIGNS (*not to scale*)
(a) C 14 tile in Haccombe Chapel, Devon.
(b) C 14 quadrant tile at Stanton St. John Church, Oxfordshire.
(c) C 14 tile, also from Stanton St. John, one of set of four forming a circular pattern in any direction.
(d) Tile of after 1398 (foundation date) at Mountgrace Priory, Yorkshire.
(e) Later mediaeval tile at Cookham-on-Thames Church, Berkshire.
(f) C 14 tile found at Butley Priory, Suffolk.
(g) C 14 tile at East Shefford Church, Berkshire—a Wessex derived design, as found at Romsey, Hampshire.
(h) Tile at St. Albans Abbey, Hertfordshire.
(i) Later mediaeval Penn-style tile originally at Ashridge, and now in Aldbury Church, Hertfordshire, with fleur-de-lis and 'fretty'.

a, b

c

4   FLEUR-DE-LIS, EARLIER AND LATER VERSIONS
(a) (b) Thirteenth-century quadrant tiles, 6 inches square, from Keynsham Abbey, Somerset. (Victoria and Albert Museum.)
(c) Mid fifteenth-century tile, 6 inches square, set diagonally, at Strensham Church, Worcestershire.

8

5   PARTI-COLOURED FLEUR-DE-LIS
Early sixteenth-century inlaid tile, $5\frac{7}{8}$ inches square, from Hailes Abbey, Gloucestershire, commissioned by Abbot Melton. (British Museum.)

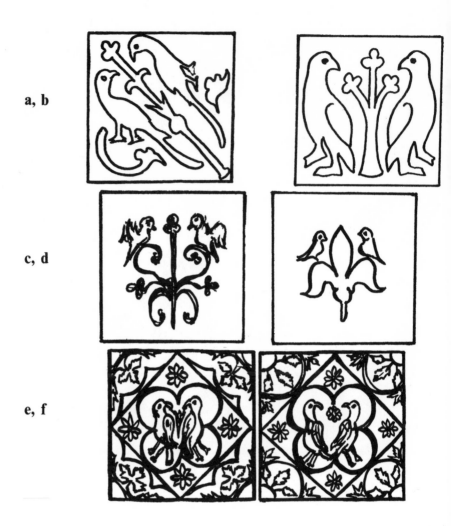

a, b

c, d

e, f

6   'TREE' AND BIRD DESIGNS (*not to scale*)
(a) Late C 13 Wessex tile, with one damaged foliage motif (example in British Museum).
(b) C 14 tile found at Butley Priory, Suffolk.
(c) (d) Later mediaeval tiles at St. Albans Abbey, Hertfordshire.
(e) (f) Late C 13 or early C 14 tiles at Titchfield Abbey, Hampshire, with foliage.
Pairs of birds are often shown 'addorsed' or back-to-back. The 'tree'—as in (a) and (b)—is an elongated fleur-de-lis.

10

is demonstrated in the plain geometry of light and dark triangles (*gyrons*) as well as in more ambitious designs like the fine heraldic lions at Ewelme and Swyncombe in Oxfordshire – the two-tailed lion of the Burghersh family – or the mermaids elsewhere whose tails curl round their tiles like a partial border. The Victorians reproduced many of these commoner tiles, but with such hard exactness – partly achieved by using plaster dies – that their charm was lost.

This talk of the common should not give any impression of restriction of subject. Loyd Haberly once began to list the designs found in the Oxford area, and stopped at 'C' only. This was his unfinished list: 'Alphabets, anchors, angels, apes, arches, barrels, battle-axes, bears, bells, birds, butterflies, capstans, carp, castles, centaurs, chequers, chevrons, children, churches, cocks, conies (rabbits), crosses ...' Not exactly 'all human life is there', but an indication of far richer variety than we might expect, given the context of the floor.

One should not overstate the contrast between the unostentatious, technically-accomplished mosaic of the ascetic Cistercian order – mosaic known, in amounts great or small, from Little Coggeshall (Essex) and Old Warden (Bedfordshire) to the great abbeys of Rievaulx and Melrose – and these mixed and multifarious later mediaeval inlays. The break is not abrupt. The twelfth-century pavement at Byland Abbey has already some small inlaid flowers. The fourteenth-century pavement in Prior Crauden's chapel, which belonged to the Benedictine house of Ely, has inlaid border tiles but is still composed mainly of traditional mosaic. Some of the Ely mosaic tiles are marked with line-impressed flowers and lions' faces. Icklingham All Saints church in Suffolk also has mosaic of this type, with still more line-impressed patterns. More important than the transitional meeting of techniques, perhaps, is the absence of any clear cultural distinction: we cannot say, for instance, that the plain mosaic was religious *in content* or that the appearance of motifs and pictures on the much more widely distributed inlaid tiles represents a secularisation or even just a fall from spiritual severity.

Large numbers, if not the bulk, of the figured tiles carry religious motifs such as ecclesiastical figures, emblems of the Passion, the Virgin's fleur-de-lis, or Christian monograms and symbols, like the fish on its oval ground or *vesica*. Their purpose, like that of the unfigured mosaic, was to ornament the floor of God's house.

St. Bernard of Clairvaux's indignation had been quite lonely, when

11

he raged with an intellectual's incomprehension – though he was also an enemy of intellectual speculation – against images and stone-carved monsters especially: 'For God's sake, if men are not ashamed of these follies, why at least do they not shrink from the expense?' (letter to the abbot of St. Thierry, about 1125). Interestingly, there appear on Wessex tiles hypnotic arabesques like those employed by the Sunni or orthodox Muslims, who rejected all images. For figured tiles monkey designs were as acceptable as crosses and church bells. Mediaeval people, after all, thought it appropriate to praise or thank God by dancing in churchyard or church, and there exists the ideal and popular story of the jongleur of Notre-Dame – Our Lady's tumbler, sweaty-browed before the altar. There were saints like the unpropertied St. Francis of Assisi and St. Roch, marked with pilgrim's sores. Men rich enough to be the donors of murals were careful to crowd representatives of every social class, even bishops, into the literally monstrous gaping jaws of Hell.

Symbols for Christ and the Virgin Mary – crowned monograms for both, the lily pot of the Annunciation for the Virgin and for Christ the fish (a rebus or punning symbol), the *Agnus Dei* or Lamb of God (used as the Templars' badge) and the pelican vulning (wounding) itself to feed its young – are not uncommon on tiles. Fleurs-de-lis, introduced as the device of the Virgin Mary, are multitudinous and supremely decorative. There is an odd dearth among the designs, though, of signs or symbols for saints–odd considering their prevalence in contemporary painting and glass and in stone and wood carvings in churches. On the panel paintings of saints on church screens, however, may be found two different types of design unusually close to tile designs. First there were the tiny squared or diaper patterns (of plaster gesso, or just painted) of the background, with geometrical or flower forms or birds. Then, later, there were larger stencilled motifs—the Virgin's and saints' monograms (like figure 38), the pelican, stylised plants and so on – which constitute a cut-out, two-dimensional patterning and the closest parallel to inlaid tile designing. Rare saintly exceptions among the tiles are the Midlands crossed keys of St. Peter or the papacy and possible Catherine wheels for the saint broken on the wheel.

Some signs are ambiguous, hovering between religion and magic, like the three rabbits or hares linked by their shared ears, that may act as a symbol of the Holy Trinity. In *The Leaping Hare* by George

Ewart Evans and David Thomson (1972) it is pointed out that these are correctly hares, 'joined in a kind of animated Catherine-wheel' and 'another instance of a pre-Christian symbol being adopted by the church'. (On roof bosses in the Dartmoor churches, financed by money from the stanneries or mines, the creatures appear as the craft-badge of the tin miners.) This 'Holy Trinity' is found on tiles in Chester Cathedral and in Buckinghamshire. The undeciphered Midlands inscription WGWER or REWGW is said to be pure magic. We can find the pagan face of the jack-of-the-green or green man, and may wonder whether the common fantasticated lions' faces are symbolic or just ornamental.

If decipherable, inscribed tiles may prove theologically unsound, like the repetitive Malvern charm against fire. The earlier Lombardic letters, used at Chertsey and Clarendon, are legible and so are the rarer curvilinear scripts – exemplified by the Bawsey memorial tile for 'Thomus' (fourteenth-century) and the Thornbury Castle Garter motto (sixteenth-century). The message of the inscriptions has often been lost, whether from disturbed single-letter tiles – as at Buckland-in-the-Moor, Devon – or through the decorative illegibility of the highly formalised Black Letter or Gothic script. Malvern's are unusually clear, but elsewhere Black Letter inscriptions, at their worst on tiles, may look like shorthand signs with meaning only for mediaeval literates. The Midlands makers actually supplied alphabet tiles, often with pre-printing mistakes in the cutting of their stamps. Even when a message is clear and obviously sound, though, it may need further interpretation. The apparently general admonition 'Have Mynde', or be careful, which is found on tiles of about 1390 in the Hospital of St. Cross and in Winchester Cathedral, must be taken as a more specific and menacing *memento mori*: its implication, instantly clear to a mediaeval bedesman, is 'remember you will die and be judged'.

The favoured secular coats-of-arms, blazons and badges could be said to appear on church floors in the way that they did on glass or panels (with or without the figures of the donors), originally identifying lay benefactors. The arms or rebuses of dioceses or bishops and abbots appear on tiles too. The surprising near-absentees, though, are the identifying marks of the merchants (used, for example, on bales), which were so often employed as a kind of heraldry – even on shields – on tombs and to label large benefactions. The spread of

13

figured tiles to lay buildings was a later mediaeval development, naturally mainly of secular content – though there are house chapels, like that of Broughton Castle in Oxfordshire, that have figured tiles. This expansion resulted partly from economic growth, and church donors might now have the funds to pave the nave floor as well as that of sanctuary and chancel, if those had been the first, limited achievement. Partly as a consequence of the Black Death's toll of craftsmen, it seems that pavements were increasingly standardised and the quicker process of 'printing' tiles was invented.

We may note here that the common survival of a group of tiles round the font may be due as much to this being a sacramental area as to its continued freedom from pews. Thus it is always worth looking for tiles near the font, where they may also have been re-set in modern times. At Long Wittenham (Berkshire), for example, the remains of two generations of tiles are collected by the Norman lead font: there are big late-mediaeval tiles, with an unusual inscribed design, and a few older and finer tiles, classic 'Wessex' inlays with birds and fleurs-de-lis.

It is the secular floors that have almost completely disappeared, though there are records of the making of tiled floors for the greatest laymen, from Henry III at Westminster and Clarendon (Wiltshire) in the thirteenth century, to Henry VIII at Hampton Court in the 1530s. Excavation has uncovered decorated tiles laid for Edward the Black Prince in the fourteenth century at his manor at Princes Risborough (Buckinghamshire) and imported tiles laid for Thomas Wolsey at the Manor of the More, near Rickmansworth (Hertfordshire), in the early sixteenth century. Numerous later mediaeval tiles from lay as well as church sites have been found in London. Exceptional secular survivals are the fourteenth-century floors discovered in 1960 at Clifton House, King's Lynn (Norfolk); the fifteenth-century Canynges' pavement from Bristol, complete but for long undisplayed, at the British Museum; and the ornate and complex Renaissance tiles at Lacock Abbey in Wiltshire, which are of the sixteenth century and were laid after the Dissolution. These are, however, very few examples to set beside the hundreds of tiles of all conditions remaining in the parish churches. These may have suffered wear, but their sites have less often been threatened with abandonment, redevelopment or redecoration.

Apart from those few secular floors, you cannot neatly subtract the spiritual from the lay: you cannot dogmatically identify the cultural source and purpose of all designs. Indeed, Nichols in 1845 quoted happily an early thirteenth-century French record which showed that the Cistercians, who followed a strict Benedictine rule, did not always maintain either their mosaic or their ascetic isolation. We should note that the order's reformist co-founder, St. Bernard, was not an iconoclast as such, but he attacked the 'grotesque and meaningless ornaments', the 'irrelevant and fanciful drollery' that had become fashionable in churches. He was not opposed to didactic art but to 'profane and meaningless paintings'. The first house, at Citeaux in France, was founded at the end of the eleventh century. In England, Rievaulx Abbey was founded in 1132, under Bernard's guidance. The fine and influential architecture of the English Cistercian houses is known from their ruins. It is clear that decorative efforts were usually rejected. At first the Cistercians had forbidden the use of any ornamentation in their churches, but the ban was later relaxed and the green and grey and yellow mosaic paving—of Byland and Rievaulx, for example—is itself evidence of this. The tile-making fitted in with the order's emphasis on physical work and industry. In their lonely sites the monasteries had to be self-supporting, but the sheep-farming of the Yorkshire Cistercians extended far beyond need, even to exports, and they developed local industries such as mining for metals.

The French record of tile-making (noted in the *Thesaurus Anecdotorum* of Martini) is doubly interesting, for it reveals both some friction over ornament and also how far that craft had developed by the thirteenth century in France—in contrast to England. It was as early as 1210 that 'slight penance' was enjoined on the Abbot of Beaubec in Normandy because he had 'for a long time' allowed one of the brethren, a maker of pavements, to work for persons not of the Cistercian order. These persons had employed the monk in making pavements inconsistent, from their 'levity and curiosity', with the gravity of the order. In future, it was ruled, he was to work only for the Cistercians, 'with whom let him not presume to construct pavements which do not extend the dignity of the order'. Obviously only figured tiles, not mere mosaic, could have achieved such profanity.

If domestic floors have been lost, so, of course, have notable ecclesiastical pavements. Some of these we know about from Victorian literature. Henry Shaw's *Specimens of Tile Pavements*, which was

15

published in 1858, included reproductions of these pavements which have since, alas, disappeared: a rose or wheel mosaic in Great Bedwyn Church, Wiltshire; fine, locally-made fifteenth-century tiles, most with heraldic designs, at Worcester Cathedral; the Chapter House floor of Salisbury Cathedral, paved with thirteenth-century Wessex tiles (resembling the worn later ones at Winchester Cathedral), replaced in about 1870. We may contrast the detailed mid-nineteenth-century literature with the subsequent, and often still Victorian, destruction of the tiles. The Victorians also made their copies of mediaeval tiles and paved hundreds of churches with them. Nichols' *Examples of Decorative Tiles* (1845) was intended to inspire the production of new patterns, it being 'the more laudable to form original designs in the spirit of ancient art' than to copy, but he recorded that people were already using the 'ready-made patterns' of mediaeval floors.

There was an odd ambivalence in the Victorian treatment of the old tiles. On the one hand exact drawings were made; on the other hand these very tiles might be destroyed in a few years' time, as happened in the Salisbury Chapter House, where tiles in good condition were replaced by Victorian copies! The Cathedral has elsewhere a few surviving tiles with perfectly clear designs. Ironically, Shaw's work must have been used for the plan of the new and un-necessary pavement. There resulted what Alec Clifton-Taylor has succinctly described as 'a detestable glazed floor'.

A typical small Victorian dispersal occurred in 1852, when figured tiles were discovered in the ruined chantry chapel on the south side of Harpsden Church in Oxfordshire. Some 'fretted' (knotted) foliage tiles were relaid in the church porch, but the Rev. I. K. Leighton gave the greater number of the tiles to the British Museum. These designs were of fretty, *gyrons* (triangles) and several hunting scenes, including a hunting dog scenting its quarry among oak leaves. This dog is also found among framed tiles at Reading's Greyfriars Church, while Rotherfield Greys Church has some similar foliage tiles – also re-set in its north porch.

In both the nineteenth and the twentieth centuries tiles in *private* collections have been at the greatest risk, particularly of being thrown away when the original collector died. This appeared to have happened to Penn-type tiles that were dug up at Hurley Priory in Berkshire in the 1930s, when some illustrations of them were published, but

16

Dr. A. B. Emden has told me their slightly more complicated fate: they were finally kept in a barn, at Cockpole Green, that was destroyed by fire and were abandoned in the rubble. In an article on the Winchester Cathedral tiles (see Booklist) G. E. C. Knapp refers to mediaeval tile fragments dug up in 1955 in the garden of the vicarage at Preston Candover (Hampshire), which certainly derived from the 'rubbish' from the archaeological collections of the Rev. Sumner Wilson, thrown away in the 1890s after Wilson's death.

Even tiles that in the past reached the sanctuary of museums via some private collection quite often did so without the vital record of their original location. This applies not just to provincial museums, like that of Colchester in Essex, but to the London museums. It is also difficult to check whether tiles have survived in places not normally open to the public. I have failed to discover, for example, whether the many figured tiles found in the 1890s at Dale Abbey in Derbyshire, and put in a 'small museum at the site', still exist – though the British Museum has some examples from Dale. Fortunately, the huge collection – including whole pavements of Cistercian mosaic from Yorkshire – made by John Manners, ninth Duke of Rutland, ended up in the British Museum.

The obvious methods of preserving uprooted tiles inside the parish church or cathedral, instead of giving or throwing them away, seem seldom to have been used. They could have been relaid in the less-used side chapels or in recesses, as was done with tiles collected up in St. Albans Cathedral and placed, mostly, below windows in the north transept. Framed examples could have been displayed, as was conscientiously done with tiles and tile fragments from the abbey site next to Winchcombe Church in Gloucestershire. Display cases, though, are preferable to setting tiles in cement or even concrete. Much more often in the past it has been memorial brasses that were prised from the floor and tacked onto walls, where the metal deteriorates through the action of damp and lime: tiles, too, set in a bad wall can deteriorate.

There had been pre-Victorian destroyers also. First, but undetectably, may have been the same Protestant iconoclasts who scratched or scraped offending words and images from the memorial brasses and erased saints' faces and emblems from the painted screens. At any period the tidying away of old tiles may have seemed, or been, desirable. There were the Puritan and other reformers to do this.

17

There were, perhaps most importantly, suave eighteenth-century purists, disdainful of any primitive 'Gothic' work. Some Victorians, not deliberate vandals, perhaps only killed the thing they loved in the course of imitation or of purposeful improvements. Yet wear, particularly of the more vulnerable mosaic, inlaid mosaic and relief tiles, must have accounted for many of the losses before, during and after the long Victorian era. In the case of the inlaid tiles, if the glaze wears away, it is the *slow* beginning of the end of the design too.

How surprising the survivals are. Take the Bordesley Abbey pavement of about 10 by 8 feet at St. Stephen's Church in Redditch (Worcestershire) and some more inlaid tiles found during the new excavation of the abbey site in 1968. Immediately after the Dissolution of the Lesser Monasteries in 1536 the removal of the tiles had begun, though obviously for domestic re-use. One of Henry VIII's receivers-general was able to produce for Richard Rich a list of the quick and unofficial sales that had been made of Bordesley Abbey property, to the benefit of local landowners. Rich was the first Chancellor of the Court of Augmentations, set up in 1536 to dispose of the monastic lands and goods. The list included these items: 'sold to Mr. Markham the old broken tile house of the reddyche' (the abbey was at Tarde-brigge, a mile from Redditch) 'and a little house by the same . . . 7s. 6d.'; 'sold to Mr. Markham the paving tile of the north side of the cloister . . . 5s.'; 'the pavement of the east side of the cloister sold to a servant of the bishop of Winchester . . . 5s.'. The bishop of Winchester at this date was Stephen Gardiner, who supported Henry VIII but was to oppose the extreme doctrinal changes and greater iconoclasm of Edward VI's reign. The mention of the 'tile house' or kiln shows us that this Cistercian abbey had made its own tiles. The pavement now in St. Stephen's vestry was laid there in the nineteenth century, the abbey site having been excavated in 1866. (The Bordesley list is printed in G. H. Cook's *Letters to Cromwell and others on the Suppression of the Monasteries*, John Baker, 1965.) There are other records of the sale of great numbers of tiles at low prices from Reading Abbey, their survivors also having been found in excavations.

Removals of tiles have continued, for various reasons, ever since the Henrician Reformation. Various people, including the less conscientious or enlightened excavators, have absorbed tiles into their own collections. This may have meant the tiles ended up in summer-houses or gardens, or in dustbins. I have read of a particularly stark

18

example of modern vandalism, perpetrated at the Norman and later-mediaeval parish church of Turville, in the Chilterns area of Buckinghamshire. In order to level it up with the churchyard, the church floor was 'flooded' with *concrete* which covered tiles and brasses and memorial slabs. Neglect is still common and indifference almost customary. One rector might speak for many in saying this: 'I am glad to know that you are interested because I have found it very difficult to persuade the parish that the tiles are as great a treasure as the mediaeval glass and brasses. Little care has been taken of them because their value was less obvious but some of the designs are very charming'. (Other rectors, probably with doctrinal right, resent being cast in the non-pastoral rôle of museum curator.) The Church of England churches have the great store of tiles. One hopes that modern interest in design generally and a specific new concern for tiles shown by 'post-Christian church trotters' and others will help parishioners save these tiles. We seem to have seen the light about mediaeval paintings, glass and brasses, but we could treat the admittedly humbler creation of tiles with greater respect.

CHAPTER TWO

Victorian revision

To consider the treatment of mediaeval tiles during the long Victorian age is important for our study of them. Faced with battered and neglected floors in many churches, paved with mixed and patched materials, pious Victorians were probably the greatest removers of old decorated tiles. Many must have been so worn that they deserved only that fate, though we know that some really good pavements were destroyed, such as the fifteenth-century tiles once in Worcester Cathedral's Singing School. Frank Renaud, who in 1892 recorded gratefully the 'wise resolve' of a former dean of Gloucester in declining the 'proffered substitute of a marble pavement' for the fifteenth-century tiles in the cathedral's sanctuary, had elsewhere encountered – during twenty years of study – far too much 'heedless and causeless destruction by persons interested in church restorations'. The destruction, however, was less influential than the copying of the old designs for new floors, for the Victorian versions of these designs have acted as a kind of filter and have actually affected and blunted our perception of the originals. The mechanical mass copying of the old tiles, good ones or bad, I believe has diminished them in our eyes – even though it was done so long ago, and always excepting the undiminishable *prima donna* floor of Westminster Abbey Chapter House.

The leading producers in this line were Mintons of Stoke-on-Trent. The firm began experiments with tile-making probably in 1828, but their first known catalogue of encaustic tiles dates from 1835. It contained sixty-two new designs. Ninety-six Minton replicas of mediaeval tiles were presented in the catalogue, *Examples of Old English Tiles,* which was first published in 1842. (The Victoria & Albert Museum has a copy.) Replicas of the pictorial tiles from Westminster, including the Confessor tile, were available from that date. They had already been included in the Temple Church pavement in London, laid in 1841, the firm's first important tiling job. The catalogue, however, also offered 'Old English' geometrical and foliage patterns, which must have seemed the pleasant and safe choice to many rectors, as well as simple religious symbols. Mintons went on using mediaeval designs, but with increasing freedom. This can be illustrated by heavy six-inch square floor tiles of 1870 (dated by their registration mark): they have, on a white ground, black and beige motifs – stylised foliage and a miniature *repeating* version of the Wessex and Malvern design of a fish in an oval.

The variety of the surviving copies of old tiles shows that the firm was willing to satisfy special orders. Their adaptability is made clear in a 'copy' letter of 1847, quoted by Geoffrey Godden in *Minton Pottery and Porcelain of the First Period* (1968). Three different fleur-de-lis designs, the most favoured mediaeval motif, were offered to a customer, but fresh designs would be submitted – if desired – according to his own idea for a 'panelled room'.

The firm of Mintons had been established in 1793 by Thomas Minton, but it was Herbert Minton the son who greatly expanded it, popularised decorative tiles and became one of Samuel Smiles' model and savagely industrious heroes. Smiles in the best-selling *Self-Help,* first published in 1859, described Herbert Minton thus: 'Mr. Minton was not so much a highly educated man, nor an economist, nor inventor, as characterised by the inexhaustible activity and ceaseless energy which he brought to bear upon the creation of a colossal business, employing some 1500 skilled artisans...' He showed different kinds of ceramic work at the Paris Exhibition of 1851 as well as in London. Minton's sales campaign gained orders from royalty and the 'nobility', succeeding best with the two-colour encaustic tiles pioneered in the 1840s. Magazine articles, as well as the aristocratic example, made tiles fashionable with the growing middle classes too, as Julian Barnard stresses in his book on *Victorian Ceramic Tiles* (1972).

They were used most often in the halls and long passages of the big Victorian houses and in the modest porches of terrace houses.

21

C

They were laid in greater numbers in churches and cathedrals. Godden has a summary, perhaps unintentionally funny: 'Messrs Mintons' tiles were, of course, world famous and examples may be found in countless Stately Houses, Churches, Railway Stations, etc.' The language of Victorian catalogues was hopefully, indiscriminately and successfully expansive. A Maws catalogue advocated tiles, 'Encaustic, Geometric, Mosaic etc. for Halls, Corridors, Passages, Conservatories, Churches, Cemetery Chapels, Porches, Gangways, Footpaths, Porticoes, Verandas, Balconies, Ships Galleys etc'. Other Staffordshire firms quickly imitated Minton and Co., who traded also from 1845 to 1875 under the name of Minton and Hollins. The history of the name Minton, though, is very complicated (with an important law suit in 1875) and Minton, Hollins continued separately until 1962. Their efforts must account for the particular paucity of mediaeval tiles in Staffordshire, where a very small number are distributed between half a dozen churches only. Along with Mintons, Maws of Broseley and Copelands were the biggest tile-producers. Other makers who imitated mediaeval tiles were William Godwin of Hereford and the Campbell Tile Co.

The tile boom is illustrated by the history of T. & R. Boote of Burslem, Staffordshire: the firm was set up in 1850 in the premises of an earlier general ceramics firm, but significantly soon became tile specialists, selling all sorts of tiles – including 'majolica' – in this country and North America. Wall-tiles, which were made thinner, could be bought in the 1840s, but were irresistibly fashionable only from 1870. In Dorset, for example, the Poole Pottery was founded in 1873 to make plain floor tiles, but soon added decorated wall-tiles. During the last quarter of the nineteenth century there were some eighty firms producing decorative tiles. The general demand tailed off only at the turn of the century, and Mintons themselves stopped making decorated tiles in about 1910.

The commercial success must have constituted a cultural overkill, which was to make even the subject of tiles unpopular afterwards – rather as the more limited Victorian interest in church brasses and brass-rubbing (and in imitating panel-type brasses for new memorials) shrank away into a small minority concern thought of as an esoteric, or even eccentric, interest until recent years. Perhaps significantly, Victorian tiles are some of the last items of Victoriana to be studied and collected. Above all, no modern general or popular study has been made of the mediaeval English tiles which were frequently their inspiration and harshly-treated originals. This is so despite the fact that decorated tiles – many with Continental mediaeval designs – are now again fashionable. We can note here, though, that the great difficulty of photographing them well has contributed to the continuing neglect of tiles. Both with black and white and with colour photography the main problem is to reproduce without reflection the effect of their uneven glaze.

The Victorian firms concentrated on making replicas of the old inlaid or printed tiles, which they called 'encaustic', as they were of two colours. Usually the design was done in white-firing clay set in a body of red-firing clay, but sometimes the Victorian tiles were done in buff and black or chocolate instead. The later tendency was for the darker colour to be inlaid. 'Encaustic' is derived from words meaning 'burning in'. Mrs. E. S. Eames (in *Medieval Tiles – A Handbook*, British Museum, 1968) points to the misuse of the term, which should be limited to enamel work: 'This method produced the tiles which most nineteenth-century writers called "encaustic", an unfortunate choice of terms because no enamels were used.' Since, however, 'encaustic' has been used to describe two-clay tiles for so long, and is so defined in the *Oxford Dictionary*, it must be taken as having been successfully subjected to the common broadening of once-specialist terms. The alternative term of 'polychrome' is inaccurate for these tiles of two rather than *many* colours, and it would be too testing always to have to distinguish between genuine inlaid and the later stamped or 'printed' mediaeval tiles (see Chapter 3, section 2c and d). The rather cumbrous description 'figured slip tiles' could take us out of this difficulty.

Inexactness of terminology, combined with a new interest in tiles, was not limited to England. A well-illustrated French book by Emile Amé was entitled *Les Carrelages Emaillés du Moyen-Age et de la Renaissance* – that is, 'The Enamelled Paving Tiles of the Middle Ages and the Renaissance'. This was published in Paris in 1859. *Emaillé*, enamelled, had its origin in the Old French word for smelting metals, but perhaps the shiny glazes of the tiles made them seem not too far removed from enamel inlays.

Samuel Smiles praised the great ceramics entrepreneur particularly because 'In perfecting these several branches Mr. Minton had many difficulties to encounter . . . and at length left even the best of the ancient tiles far behind'. The multiplication of the demand for decorated tiles finally led to most being printed by transfer, but the 'Old English' designs were made with plaster dies and no, or shallow, leadless glaze. Minton's was a technical achievement, the aesthetic result of which in the copies is often distasteful. Designs were carefully and efficiently reproduced: the effect was lost because the mediaeval variety of colouring and general unevenness disappeared. A. B. Emden has spoken of the 'grim uniformity' of the Victorian tiles. Mintons could achieve not only mechanical pressing and cutting, with a plaster-died precision for the inlays, but incomparably more efficient firing and an exactness of colouring that completely eluded the mediaeval potters and tilers. In the old work, irregularities of colouring and glaze as well as of line are normal. They were derived from impurities in the glaze material or its uneven distribution. Mediaeval tiles could be speckled or mottled from the iron content of the clay body. Salts could come to the surface during the single firing and be held there by the glaze, forming whitish or grey patches – ugly if at all obvious. Oxidisation varied, glazes staying dark when there was less oxygen in the kiln. It is true that these irregularities were not intended as an integral part of the design, but many of the smaller ones help make the tiles easy on the eye. Even the fine inlays of the Westminster Chapter House tiles lie under glazes that are not just rich but uneven.

The Victorian replicas were only in some senses too good. They removed all patchiness of colouring, in favour of hard yellows or sour cream and dead browns or chestnut, but they still copied the irregularities of line of their originals, unavoidably, and the combination can be comic or even ludicrous. The copies of a later mediaeval tile design of a rampant lion laid in the entrance to the Westminster Abbey Chapter House exemplify this oddness: why, one now asks, has the lion one rectangular eye and one triangular eye and what is his angular football? (Figure 10.) The Minton copies of the Chapter House tiles, including the popular Confessor design, just look heavier and duller than did their mid-thirteenth-century originals – that were presumably 'the best of the ancient tiles'. The copies were first produced when the Chapter House pavement was still normally invisible, being covered over with boards, so that the designs were a revelation to almost everyone. Herbert Minton collected old tiles himself, and the collection was augmented by examples – or sketches of them – that were sent to him when his interest became known.

24

The most honourable exceptions to the Victorian hardness of colouring tended to come when firms used modern, but appropriate, colours and relied on the mediaeval designs for free inspiration only. The Houses of Parliament, for instance, have some Victorian six-inch tiles with heraldic badges done in unglazed cream, beige and strong sky blue. The designs – some of the mediaeval royal beasts – and colours are new and very attractive and the tiles were designed by A. W. N. Pugin, the architect, and made by Mintons.

Another firm which began to create replicas of mediaeval tiles at the start of the tile-making revival was that of William Godwin of Hereford. This firm was established at the Lugwardine Works, three miles east of Hereford, in 1848. Llewellyn Jewitt, author of *Ceramic Art of Great Britain* (1878), seems to have mistaken an expansion at Withington for the firm's foundation, dating this at 1861. The tiles had already won an award at an exhibition at Adelaide, Australia, in 1857. Godwin claimed to have made at Lugwardine the first dust-pressed tiles – that is, made of reconstituted clay, and therefore dense and even in texture. Mintons themselves, the most famous producers, were to take out patents for several different methods of dust-pressed manufacture – the first about 1850. (The clay was par-dried and various substances might be added.) In 1868 Godwin erected new works for dust-pressed tiles at Whitestone, close to Lugwardine. Whitestone is still the location of the successor company Hereford Tiles Ltd., whose machines produce tiles 'in over a hundred colours'. Mintons has been absorbed into Doultons, but had stopped making tiles before the First World War, while 'most of the Victorian and later tile manufacturers . . . eventually found their way into the present H & R Johnson-Richards Tiles group' of Stoke-on-Trent. These included T & R Boote of Burslem (taken over in 1963) who patented a dust processing method in 1863, and the Minton, Hollins firm (taken over in 1962).

It is noteworthy that William Godwin's was a specialised firm, making 'encaustic' floor tiles to new and old designs and soon also wall-tiles. Minton, Hollins was initiated in 1845 simply as the tile section of the ceramics firm. Even the Campbell Tile Company, established in 1875, whose tiles ranged from reproduction 'Romano-British' mosaic to 'majolica' and painted wall-tiles of foliage and wild flowers, was properly The Campbell Brick and Tile Company.

Edward Welby Pugin set Godwin tiles in the new Benedictine

monastery at Hereford in 1856, and himself designed new tiles for Minton-Hollins and the Campbell Tile Company, both at Stoke-on-Trent. Pugin junior, at the age of seventeen, had taken over the practice of his father, the great Catholic architect A. W. N. Pugin. In the opinion of the architect Sir George Gilbert Scott, recorded in his *Personal and Professional Recollections* (published posthumously in 1879), Godwins of Hereford made the best replica tiles. Scott, advocate and practitioner of the Gothic Revival, was the familiar mixture of drastic restorer and genuine student of the mediaeval. One example of his employment of Godwin tiles is at Milton Abbas in Dorset (see below). These tiles' success must have been aided by the rich colouring of the red Herefordshire clay. Llewellyn Jewitt noted that Godwin aimed to achieve 'perfect facsimiles' through the 'correctness' of their design as well as – interestingly and unusually – an 'antique appearance of surface'. The replicas were typically small, four or four-and-a-half inches square. In the domestic context Charles Eastlake, in the influential *Hints on Household Taste* (published 1868; fourth edition 1878) commended Godwin tiles for colour and design, but Maws' for variety and 'technical accomplishment'. Maws' range is well illustrated by two fantastic bays at Worcester's Shrub Hill Station.

The most prolific tile-producers were to be Maws of the Benthall Works, near Broseley, an industrial and clay pipe town. These works were in the Ironbridge Gorge of Shropshire, where they were joined by Craven Dunhill, an independent tile firm which operated from 1872 to 1951 and marked its goods with a trademark of bottle kilns. The local clay fired a paler red than the Hereford company's. Maws made some comparatively large mediaeval-style tiles, seven inches square. The origins of this firm were particularly important for the replica trade. The firm moved to Broseley in 1852, but had started up in 1850 with the acquistion of the Worcester firm of Frederick St. John, George Barr and Co. That firm had issued a catalogue of seventy-seven mediaeval designs in 1844. They copied, for example, the fine early sixteenth-century heraldic tiles found at Thornbury Castle in Gloucestershire. Albert Way, writing about the mediaeval tiles at Great Malvern Priory in *The Gentleman's Magazine* for May 1844, had strong praise for this firm's 'very successful revival' of tile manufacture and boasted that 'revived taste... renders pavements of decorative tiles daily in request'. We may mention here that the porcelain firm of Chamberlains of Worcester (wound up in 1852) made some rare and exact copies of Malvern foliage tiles – beautiful, highly-glazed and, if they were for the floor, impractical.

As noted, Herbert Minton had initiated some abortive experiments in copying mediaeval tiles in 1828 and returned to the project a few years later. In the interval, in 1830, a patent for imitating mediaeval tiles was taken out by a stray, unbusinesslike enthusiast, Samuel Wright of Shelton, Staffordshire. It was specified that he would use plaster dies for making the designs and metallic oxides for colouring the clays. In the mediaeval tiles the metallic oxides were used for the glaze, the clays not being coloured. Wright was not successful commercially and finally disposed of the patent, under separate conditions, to Herbert Minton of Stoke and George Barr of Worcester. Here, then, is our hidden *fons et origo* of replica-making.

For the detailed history of the Victorian firms see – as well as the Victorian Jewitt's *Ceramic Art* – the remarkable compilation by W. J. Furnival, entitled *Leadless Decorative Tiles, Faience and Mosaic* and published at Stone (Staffordshire) in 1904. This includes contributions on Indian, Asian and European tiles and on the history of tile-making, but was mainly intended as a huge practical tract against contemporary tile-makers' use of lead and includes recipes for leadless colours. Minton is presented as a hero of leadless enterprise. Furnival, who also wrote books against vaccination, saw lead still in general use although an annual average of 230 women workers, alone, suffered lead poisoning. The health of the mediaeval tilers must also have suffered, although their smaller production and relative inefficiency must have reduced the danger.

Normally Victorian copies were the exact size of their mediaeval originals, but this was sometimes changed to fit in with stock units. We can see an example of this in the mediaeval chapel of Jesus College at Cambridge, which had been the church of the nunnery dissolved at the end of the fifteenth century. From 1849 to 1851 this dilapidated building and its fittings were restored by Augustus Welby Northmore Pugin senior, the conscientious and most formidable architect of the Gothic Revival. (He died in 1852, aged only forty, after mental breakdown had caused his early retirement.) Pugin had 'mediaeval' encaustic tiles laid in the choir and under the crossing. Most of the Jesus tiles have simple patterns, such as a stocky fleur-de-lis, but a Great Malvern design of foliage in a traceried circle is included –

27

shrunk from six to four inches square. This reduction is neat, technically very accomplished, but the result is too dense and is out of scale with the rest of the pavement. Even here, where the colours are pleasant, the impact and local identity of the originals is missing. This is just one of hundreds of imitations of mediaeval pavements. The Victorian versions, even at best, are commonplace – but they may have an extrinsic value as records.

Even those who dislike or despise the Victorian replicas should not avoid looking at them, for most were conscientious copies of originals which may now have vanished – or be much more worn and indecipherable than they were in the mid-nineteenth century. Both originals and copies are, of course, still continuously at risk, so it is worthwhile tracing rare designs from both. Dr. A. B. Emden (at a conference on mediaeval tiles, held at Oxford in May 1973), has presented us with a telling example, recorded in a tracing, of the value of the Victorian revival. The example was from Sherborne in Dorset. The old Benedictine abbey church (now school chapel) has many Wessex-style mediaeval tiles and *had* also Minton replicas. Mintons had been able to copy a beautiful, unique design, seven-and-a-half inches square, for which Dr. Emden could find only four 'hardly legible' original fragments. It was a quadrant design, made to be laid in sets of four, with a typical curved band of foliage and a large compound leaf in the spandrel (corner). In the opposite corner were two fishes, with cusped or pointed fins, but the main fauna were a big-eyed heron bending down to tackle a huge eel – of conger proportions. The bird had one foot on its catch and the other raised. The stylised stance, the crest and stylised regular wing and tail feathers, all suggest hieratic Eastern art. Quite recently, though, all the Minton tiles were removed and dispersed—sold casually, given or thrown away – and puritan stone flags laid in their place.

The first important new pavement was laid in the Temple Church in the City of London in 1841 and what was done there was both anachronistic and prophetic. A 'drastic' structural renovation of the building was carried out, to be partly undone by the Blitz of 1941. To quote from *An Encyclopaedia of London*, edited by William Kent, 1937: 'The pavement was lowered about 16 in. at the same date, and at that time numerous inscribed gravestones were removed to the N. chyd. A few of the old tiles were found. Many of the present ones were designed from the remains of the old ones found there, and in the

7   Nineteenth century replica by Minton of Wessex-style inlaid quadrant tile, $7\frac{1}{2}$ inches square, from Sherborne Abbey, Dorset. (*After tracing by Dr A. B. Emden.*)

chapter house of W.A.' It was the few designs of human figures, unrepresentative of the panelled foliage and animal Westminster Abbey Chapter House pavement, which were found most attractive by Mintons and their customers – and here contributed to an odd mixture, that was in part a solid record. Sizes varied: there were the usual small quadrant tiles, one foliage design forming circles, and larger tiles with an animal motif. The few originals were evidently not preserved, and the Victorian tiles have in their turn vanished in the post-War restoration.

29

Some Victorian church pavements were wholly composed of copies of mediaeval tiles found in those particular churches, or included a number of such replicas – perhaps with a few originals being preserved as proof that this was done. One should note that, even where the old floor was the only source of the designs for a new pavement, the old layout was probably not copied. In particular, we find an excess of hard black tiles, used for groups or panel borders. Extra designs were often added, which can be detected if they were of different date or in the wrong regional style.

The plain border tiles were probably made as an improvement, to obviate some criticism of the first, wholly figured new pavements. As early as 1846 in his *Concise Glossary of Architecture* the prolific architectural historian, John Henry Parker, had critically examined the relation between the old and the new floors: 'A profusion of good examples still exists of single tiles, and sets of four, nine, sixteen, or a greater number of tiles, forming by their combination a complete design, and presenting, for the most part, the characteristic style of ornament which was in vogue at each successive period; but examples of general arrangement are very rare and imperfect. To this deficiency of authorities it seems to be due, that modern imitations of these ancient pavements have generally proved unsatisfactory, in the resemblance which they present to oil-cloth, or carpeting, and the intention of producing richness of effect by carrying the ornamental design throughout the pavement without any intervening spaces, has been wholly frustrated.' Parker saw in the new floors 'a confused rather than rich effect', whereas originally plain tiles had divided 'the various portions which composed the general design'. There is still enough evidence, though, to show that this generalisation does not hold up. Though there are plain yellow, green and blackish mediaeval border tiles, figured tiles – as at Westminster – were also used for borders and there are other floors without divisions.

The unbroken and extravagant 'oil-cloth' layout of, say, the Lady Chapel floor in A. W. N. Pugin's Roman Catholic church of St. Giles, erected in 1845–1848, at Cheadle in Staffordshire was not in essence unmediaeval. John Betjeman, in *A Pictorial History of English Architecture* (1970), labels this floor 'a maze of patterns in Minton's tiles'. As Betjeman points out, externally, buildings by Pugin were often close to the mediaeval and comparatively simple, while his interiors were ornate. There is no blank space at St. Giles, whole walls even being covered with stencilled decoration. There are trefoil-ended crosses on the walls and on the floor of the Lady Chapel. Only a large circular *Agnus Dei* (Lamb of God) design on a blue ground lacks a mediaeval tile original. The bright 'encaustic' pavement is set out in panels, with patterned divisions, and contributes to the relentlessness of the general decoration. All the same, it is mainly the mixture, not the layout, of the pavement that is anachronistic. The aggressiveness is in each single technically perfect tile, and does not disappear when the layouts are less ambitious and include modest plain borders. Even though it consists only of plain brown borders and panels with only one design – a mediaeval angular interlace with a rosette in the middle, inspired by a motif in the vaulting – the paving of the Round Church of the Holy Sepulchre at Cambridge, for instance, is so intrusive that we avert our eyes and look only at the Norman limestone. We have, in fact, become used to ignoring and forgetting many church floors.

A typical Victorian revision and restoration occurred at Milton Abbas in Dorset, when Gilbert Scott set a new floor in the parish church, once the abbey church. This had copies – made by Godwins of Hereford – of some of the old tiles, but also extra designs from elsewhere and the layout was new. Fortunately and unusually, about six hundred worn originals with fine Wessex designs were moved to another ex-monastic building, St. Catherine's Chapel, where they remain. While it was not unusual for the new tiles to be exact copies of the old, it was unusual for a whole floor of old tiles to be retained in the building – as happened at Chastleton in Oxfordshire.

Willington Church in Bedfordshire, also perhaps unusually, has quite a complicated collection of old and new. There are a few mediaeval tiles with geometric designs in the north chapel, by the organ; there are careful Victorian copies of them laid in front of the altar, with copies (I believe) of lost originals – such as a fleur-de-lis; there are also wholly new Victorian designs set in the chancel. The entry in Nikolaus Pevsner's *Buildings of England*, volume *Bedfordshire and the County of Huntingdon and Peterborough* (1968) reads: 'TILES in the chancel. They are typical of the moment after the Minton type of the mid C 19. They date from 1876–7 (restoration under *Clutton*) and are rather orientally inspired'. A footnote, contributed by G. McHardy, points out 'Also some mediaeval tiles. They are in the N chapel'. Both, however, ignore the partial correspondence between the mediaeval and Victorian tiles.

31

Tewkesbury Abbey in Gloucestershire retains a few mediaeval tiles, in recesses and chantry chapels, but has a chancel wholly paved with Victorian copies of tiles rediscovered at that period and now mostly lost. At Dorchester Abbey in Oxfordshire the surviving original tiles were evidently limited to two fragmentary strips – against the north wall of the nave and at the base of a screen between the nave and the south-west aisle which was erected for lay parishioners in the fourteenth century – but their patterns were 'followed in the Victorian tiles with which the nearby altar platform is paved' in the south-west aisle. At Wirksworth Church in Derbyshire the nineteenth-century restoration included the removal of the mediaeval patterned tiles, but the chancel was paved with copies of them, the designs including birds and butterflies. At Ashbourne Church, also in Derbyshire, about a hundred tiles were kept and are still in a cupboard in the church, while a new floor was made 'to a certain extent' copying the original.

In other places decorated tiles were probably introduced for the first time, new 'mediaeval' tiles picked from a catalogue, in the smaller churches. A little village church like Tidmarsh in Berkshire could be loaded with shining copies of some of the Westminster tiles, including the inevitable Confessor design. These were Minton tiles, as advertised in the 1842 catalogue. At Moulsford not far away (also in Berkshire) a real Minton-catalogue pavement was laid, evidently to celebrate the village's gaining of parochial status in 1846! Moulsford had a chapel, which – in the language of a marble wall memorial – was restored and considerably improved at that date. The architect was Giles Gilbert Scott. The blandly-named 'restoration' amounted to the complete rebuilding of the chapel – but on the same scale – utilising only the original west wall. The sanctuary was given an encaustic pavement, including a Westminster Abbey design of trailing foliage which was used for the borders. The rest of the pavement consisted of groups of four tiles laid diamond-wise, with plain tiles between. Another Westminster design, of little trefoils on a grid, was used but looks somehow spindly. Also employed were one or two Penn designs and a convincingly-mediaeval lamb-and-flag emblem of Christ. A cross with its arms terminating in the signs of the Evangelists does not look like a tile design, though, and could be from a manuscript or a brass, if it was not a new invention. Under the altar table are sour yellow and brown tiles with restless stringy

8   ENCAUSTIC TILE-MAKING AT WORCESTER, 1843

The illustration shows the pressing and inlaying, by hand, of two-colour tiles at the Royal Porcelain Works. This firm had been formed by the amalgamation of Flight, Barr & Barr with Chamberlain & Co. The illustration was printed with an article, mainly on Worcester porcelain, in the *Penny Magazine* for February 1843 (page 80, volume 12). Information: Dr Francis Celoria.

Reproduced by kind permission of The Guildhall Library, City of London.

quatrefoils. All in all, what must have seemed then pleasantly fashionable now seems a heavy, unhomogeneous mixture.

At Chastleton Church (Oxfordshire) there is an example of Victorian choice-making, both gentle and interesting. Four or five hundred inlaid tiles of the fifteenth century, supposedly from Droitwich, survive in the south chapel. Many of them are very worn and certainly were already worn in the nineteenth century. They were designed and laid diamond-wise and are nearly five inches square. There are about two dozen different designs and some form groups of four, nine or sixteen tiles with radiating patterns. The chancel has a Victorian pavement, consisting of copies of about a dozen mediaeval designs, with plain borders. What is interesting is which motifs were chosen and which were ignored. Rightly rejected was the one inscribed design, with the strange letters REWGW. These are probably the initial letters of an undeciphered charm, that is, a piece of witchcraft. The motif is also found in places in Warwickshire and at Bradgate House near Leicester, and there is another version reading WGWER. A single new inscribed tile was placed before the altar (right): this reads CIRCUMDABO + ALTARE + TUUM from the Latin *Vulgate,* 'I will compass (or go about) thine altar', words of personal consecration used by the priest during mass. (Psalm 26, verse vi: 'I will wash my hands in innocency, O Lord, and so will I go to thine altar' in the *Authorised Version.*)

The types of design chosen for reproduction at Chastleton were the purely decorative, mainly foliage tiles bearing such motifs as holly leaves and berries, wreathed rosettes and a flamelike pattern probably based on an opening bud of leaves. Finer versions of the two holly patterns, incidentally, are known from Bradgate House. The originals inlaid with the torch-like bud pattern, laid down in groups of four, are especially worn: two forms of the design, however, are found at Bradgate House and elsewhere, from which it appears that the Victorian version was an improvement – both tidying up and elaborating the ragged leaf edging to the tile which constitutes a cusped border. The other copies are exact. The copying of the tile sets involved the reproduction of several tiles for one or two uses only.

Rejected at Chastleton were two heraldic designs – the six covered cups of Boteler and the crosslets, probably of Beauchamp – and an attractive, unusual tile with a merchant's mark, all these being perhaps of mediaeval interest only. Probably regarded as too crude was a royal semi-grotesque: this design consists of a large king's head with grotesquely tiny arms swinging up past his ears and holding two mysterious objects, presumably sceptres – or one could be a key.

One would love to know how Victorian Chastleton's special order to the tile manufacturers was costed, but the parish is very small and one can safely assume that the 'big house' next the church paid the bill.

In the nineteenth century the English mediaeval tiles were really being looked at across an enormous gulf of time and culture, un-bridged by any continuance of traditions. The revival of tile-making was associated with the new curiosity of antiquaries about the old tiles, mostly of the fourteenth and fifteenth centuries, that survived in the churches. Both the antiquarian or archaeological interest and that of the post-Industrial Revolution 'potters' was reinforced by the first discoveries of the sites of mediaeval decorated floor tile kilns – at Malvern, Droitwich, Great Saredon, Bawsey, Repton and Dale. Investigation continued through the Victorian age. So did the mass production of glossy or matt slavish copies of floor tiles – even when new designs had been added to the repertoire – and of the smaller plain dark tiles which were so over-used for borders. The profitable tile-mania even included the paving of the railway station of Stoke-on-Trent itself, centre of the Potteries. The machines pressed out tiles often uninspired in design, but durable.

Early- and late-Victorian tile designs were carried out with a wider range of methods, materials and colours than the mediaeval makers could command, but it is usually the more elaborate mixtures that seem heavy and unattractive. Though the ones of an aggressive bright brown are both common and repellent, single-colour relief tiles are often pleasant or even admirable. The variety and quantity of the Victorian and Edwardian tiles is still so overwhelming that it is difficult to see clearly past them to the originals. There are even a surprising number of people, presumably merely because they have not really thought about the subject, who cannot distinguish between mediaeval tiles and modern copies of them – although they would not hesitate over the difference between mediaeval and modern stonework. Production of the original tiles was really ended at Henry VIII's Reformation, but had already slackened during the fifteenth century.

The erratic history of the tiles used in England includes movements against the usual trends for a craft. What happened in the Middle

Ages seems paralleled by Victorian developments. It was the mediaeval figured tiles, the relief or inlaid or 'printed' tiles, that were made 'in bulk'. There followed, from the first half of the sixteenth century, the importing of hand-painted tiles – of which the rare maiolica floor tiles of The Vyne in Hampshire were early examples. Nearly all were wall-tiles, which were also made in England. Then in the nineteenth century the Staffordshire Potteries sold tiles that were from the first machine-made, mass-produced. William Morris and William de Morgan, however, turned back to craft-style designing and actually influenced the mass-producers to more original design. It is surprising that this industry, unlike others, did not proceed simply from the hand-made and individual to the increasingly mechanised production of replicas. (Have you seen the nadir, plastic apostle teaspoons?)

It seems rather unexpected to find the mediaeval tile-makers so involved, efficiently or inefficiently, in large-scale production. Not only were commercial kilns developed, but peripatetic tilers – freed from the normal mediaeval guild restrictions – took their design stamps from area to area. There must have been many more kilns than excavation has found. The popular quadrant tiles can perhaps be held to typify production for a large, non-specialised market, mainly in the Home Counties and the Midlands. Four of these tiles laid together make a radiating pattern, each tile having the same (incomplete) motifs – very often foliage with a quarter circle or wreath. Many of these were chosen for copying in the nineteenth century.

One of the most important limitations on the mediaeval tiles, and even on the Victorian pavements, was obviously just that they were made to be trodden on. This tended to favour simplicity of line. Some of the more complex survivals may only be explained by the lesser impact of soft mediaeval shoes or sandals (as against hard modern soles and raised heels), followed by the modern desertion of the countryside and the churches. The nearest thing we can find to hand-painting is the occasional scratching of fine details on mediaeval tiles with a pointed tool. The Victorians in their turn did not waste hand-painting on floor tiles, reserving it still for special wall-tiles – as had been done in the centuries between.

a

b

9   LIONS
(a) Lion in quatrefoil: worn thirteenth- or fourteenth-century tile ($4\frac{1}{2}$ inches square)
at Canterbury Cathedral.
(b) Inlaid tile of about 1325 at Clifton House, King's Lynn, Norfolk (about $4\frac{3}{4}$ inches
square).

D

10   LION
Victorian copy of mediaeval tile (4¼ inches square) in Westminster Abbey Chapter
House antechamber.

LION'S HEAD WITH
LEAF FOR TONGUE
Five-sided tile, probably
fourteenth-century,
excavated in 1916 at the
site of the palace of the
Bishops of Salisbury at
Sonning, Berkshire.
(Sides about $3\frac{3}{4}$, $3\frac{1}{4}$ and
$2\frac{3}{4}$ inches.) Reading
Museum.

11   DOUBLE-TAILED HERALDIC LION
Fourteenth- or fifteenth-century inlaid tile (5 inches square) at Swyncombe Church,
Oxfordshire.

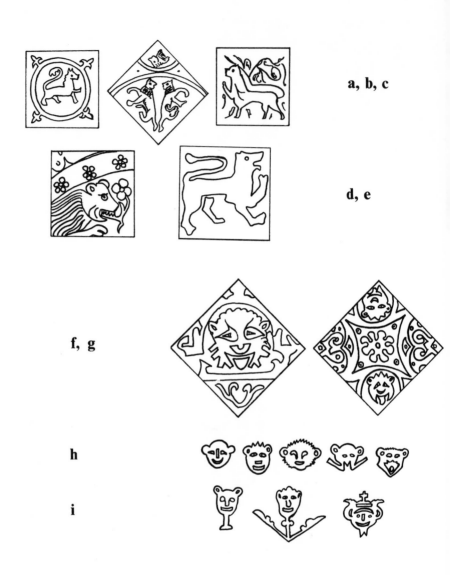

12   LIONS AND LIONS' FACES (*not to scale*)

(a) C 13 or C 14 Wessex tile.

(b) Quadrant tile in Westminster Abbey Chapter House (6 inches square), about 1255.

(c) C 14 relief tile found at Butley Priory, Suffolk. Possibly imported.

(d) Tile of lion with flower in mouth (in Victoria and Albert Museum), of Worcestershire style and designed as part of a 16-tile group.

(e) C 14 Penn-type printed tile.

(f) (g) C 14 Penn-type tiles.

(h) (i) Faces from corners of C 14 inlaid or printed tiles from Penn and other Home Counties sources.

40

CHAPTER THREE

The mediaeval varieties

1 COLOURS AND GLAZES

The mediaeval craftsmen produced decorated tiles in three main colours: glazed earthenware or self-colour, yellow, and green, which is less common. Self-colour and yellow or a darker self-colour and green could be paired, but there were no three-colour English tiles – unlike the more ornate pottery vessels. The tilers' basic colours encompassed a big range of shades. In none of them was purity achieved since the materials were impure and the firing uneven. Self-colour ranged from reddish-brown to dark chocolate, and yellow ranged from cream or primrose to dark chrome yellow, honey or old gold. The greens were the most varied, including pale bright green, grey-greens, olive and a very dark green, nearly black. In addition, but more uncertainly, a blackish or purplish-black colouring is sometimes found, besides stray blues.

The colours were produced from four substances: dark clay and pale clay, with two metals, lead and added copper. Tile colours were more limited and mundane than those used for some contemporary pottery, for foreign maiolica and for coloured glass. The most sophisticated and subtle colours were those of mediaeval glass, whether the greys and greens of the early grisaille, the rich, heavy colours of the older figured glass or the brighter, clear colours used at the end of the Middle Ages. The relationship between mediaeval glass and Victorian glass is, however, rather like that between mediaeval and Victorian tiles, the Victorian products suffering from their dead purity of materials. To obtain coloured glass, certain metallic oxides were added to the 'white' glass mix, of which the main element was sand (silica). Cobalt made blue; copper made ruby red, a colour unobtainable in ceramics; iron made green and yellow; manganese made purple. Variations in the chemicals and in temperature produced variations in the colours, while details could be painted on – or all the glass could be painted with similar pigments and some details scratched white. The 'pot metal' method of colouring glass, with all the chemicals fired together, could not give direct inspiration to tilers or others in England. Coloured glass was imported until the sixteenth century; only plain glass was made here. The earliest patent was an abortive one, granted in 1449 to a Fleming 'to make glass of all colours' for Eton College. The Eton windows were actually painted by John Prudde, glazier of the Beauchamp chantry chapel at Warwick.

Interestingly, floor tiles are often depicted in mediaeval glass, as a 'ground' for the standing figures of saints and for kneeling donors. These patches of tiles are often black and white, as in fifteenth-century glass at Exeter Cathedral, Malvern Priory (Worcestershire), All Souls' College chapel in Oxford and St. Peter Mancroft Church in Norwich. This was Continental colouring, rather than English. The window tiles could have been inspired by Italian marble floors. There is a 1411 record of the Wardens of London Bridge buying black and white tiles, but this has several possible interpretations, one that they were imports. A fifteenth-century 'Dance of Death' panel of glass in St. Andrew's Church in Norwich shows more elaborate square tiles, white ones each with a circle of black in the centre and black ones with white circles. Figured tile motifs in glass are more uncommon. There are a few late fifteenth-century examples at Shelton Church in Norfolk: they look like English tile designs and include four-lobed floral or geometrical patterns.

At Clavering Church in Essex (in the north aisle) the fine, but fragmentary painted glass of the fifteenth century has various 'tile floors', the ground for small bright figures of angels. These pictured tiles include the black-and-white pavement also seen at St. Andrews Church in Norwich, besides plain white tiles alternating with black, brown or cross-hatched squares. The most interesting painted pavement, which is shown more than once, takes us back to mosaic tiling. It consists of black-outlined circular white bands (with thin black quadrilaterals between them, where the circles do not touch) around yellow circles, each of which carries a six-petalled rosette. The whole pattern is elsewhere outlined on blue glass, for a background, reminding us that favoured designs would be used for different materials and purposes. This same pattern, as a blue background and as border tiles, is also found in the fifteenth-century glass in Long Melford Church in Suffolk. So are more dark and light squares and a black and white *gyronny* pattern (triangles). Other elaborate and colourful designs at Long Melford, however, look more like carpets than tile floors. All are provided as 'grounds' for the figures of lay donors. The Clavering and Long Melford glass was produced by the Norwich glass painters. In practice the rosettes of the circular design could have been line-impressed on tiles, like the double or triple rosettes at Prior Crauden's Chapel in Ely, or inlaid. At Clavering there are also coloured border or edging strips to the little pavements, with more rosettes and small circles. Coloured and decorated tiles were also often depicted at the feet of saints in the painted panels of church screens, but again were not necessarily English in inspiration.

At the end of the Middle Ages maiolica tiles in a glass-like range of colours were imported, but they were handpainted over a white layer of tin oxide. The colours were green, derived from copper, blue from cobalt, purple from manganese, yellow from antimony, orange and brown from iron rust, and chestnut, dark brown and black from mixed pigments. (Details from *Italian Maiolica*, John Scott-Taggart, 1972.)

The tile colours and methods of decoration are closest to pottery, but only certain elements coincide. The same lead (or lead-based) glaze was used for both and had been used for pottery since the ninth century. Later on, though, potters mixed the lead with liquid clay or slurry, a practice which caused innumerable useless wasters since the pots would stick together in the firing. Colours could be varied by varying the temperature of firing, which was lower for pottery than tiles because of the thinner walls. Some glaze mixtures were complicated enough to need recipes. The potters could produce a rich but opaque treacle-brown colour, from iron added to the glaze, which was not used with tiles. Brown tiles exist, for instance among the Bawsey relief tiles (and the seventeenth-century Devon ones) but are not common. Copper-derived greens were made in England from the thirteenth century on, but the brightest and best was a late development – now labelled 'Tudor green'. This colour is also seen on large and rare memorial tiles of the sixteenth century in Lingfield Church in Surrey. These have figures in relief. Two-colour vessels were quite common, but more colours could be used. One famous thirteenth-century jug, at the London Museum, has green trellis decoration, studded with pinky red flowers that have yellow centres. As well as using different colours, the potters striped and combed the vessels; made all sort of projections, knobs and networks; modelled animals and faces and hands; slip-painted or scraped *sgraffito* designs in slip, a technique especially useful for heraldry. Relief work was used on some tiles as well as on pottery, but knobbly floors cannot have been comfortable or sensible, and *sgraffito* tiles were evidently rare.

The pottery and tile industries were organised together. Significantly, the Cistercians, the first makers of decorative floor tiles, were also potters. At Fountains Abbey in Yorkshire traces of pottery manufacture have been found and there are surviving patches of mosaic tiling. The Cistercians produced tiles of more colours than was customary later, varying the glazes more. Manufacture of batches of tiles for wider distribution made for toughness and simplicity; whereas pottery vessels had to be made individually and were decorated by hand for the affluent. Even so, a short life would have been expected of most pots.

Practicality put limits on tile decoration and explains the provincial colouring. In the making of the different colours the glaze was the most important element, partly because of its vividness. The English tiles were fired just once, achieving a good fusion between the glaze and the earthenware body or, even better, between the glaze and the layer or inlay of slip. In the British Museum *Handbook* Mrs. Eames points out that English tiles retained more colour after wear of the glaze than did contemporary double-fired tiles made in the Netherlands, which had a glossier glaze that flaked off in wear. Fusion was aided by the uneven body texture and by the presence of grains of sand (silica) in the clay, the glaze material giving a protective glassy surface to the tiles. The glaze fired yellow through oxidisation, but was transparent if made from the plain lead ore. The main requirement was usually that it be clear, for the sake of the pattern. Colours varied because chemical purity was not attained. In addition, grey opaque blotches of salt could survive if the tiles were underfired, while lustre-like patches resulted from over-firing. There may be dark speckles on the tiles, these being atoms of iron found in the redder-firing clays, and dark specks are common in green glaze.

The lead was 'Galena', the main lead ore, in the form of a sulphide or salt (PbS). Later, lead mining would be concentrated in the northern regions, but small deposits were widespread in the British Isles. It is a silvery-grey substance, easy to crumble and was used as a powder by the tilers. They must have sprinkled it on the 'green' tiles, when these were 'leather-hard' (Bernard Rackham), or dusted it on with a rag. During the firing it melted and turned yellow, reddish-yellow or buff, but the earthenware body below makes it look several tones darker – sometimes even dark brown. The fumes must have been formidable. At a later period lead sulphide was known as 'potter's ore' or 'smithum'. One may note that liquid glazes were developed as late as the eighteenth century, when they made two firings a necessity. The brownish or self-colour glazed tiles can vary considerably in colour, for even the ore was variable. Designs in relief or counter-relief on such tiles lack sharp outlines. There are examples of brown relief tiles among the products of Bawsey (Norfolk), for example a wyvern, or dragon, design.

Plain yellow tiles were produced by coating the body with slip before glazing. The slip was wetter than the body clay and one can sometimes see scrape marks from the knife or other tool with which it was spread on. There is a clear example in a mixed collection of tiles from the lost abbey at Winchcombe, Gloucestershire, that are kept in the parish church there. Relief tiles that fired yellow were also produced by coating the whole surface with slip, but only after the raised design had been stamped on them. The two-colour inlaid or printed tiles gain their effect of a yellow inlay from the slip being so much paler than the main clay and therefore altering the tone of the glaze less.

Different greens were made by adding small quantities of copper sulphide to the lead ore. The copper particles did not mix in evenly, so green tiles are streaked and speckled. There may be thin patches, where less copper fell, or dense dark areas. Pale green was produced if the glaze mixture was used over slip. Dark greens were made either by using a higher proportion of copper in the glaze of slip tiles or by glazing the ground clay. Some greens are nearly black. It used to be suggested that the purplish-black tiles sometimes found had added manganese, but – as is pointed out in the British Museum *Handbook* – recent chemical analysis has normally found only a higher copper content. Manganese may have been included accidentally, since the

a, b

c, d

13　FLORA AND FAUNA
(a) to (c) C 14 tiles, $4\frac{1}{2}$ inches square, with Buckinghamshire-style hunting designs.
(a) Hunting dog, Greyfriars Church, Reading.
(b) Running hare, Greyfriars Church, Reading.
(c) Sitting rabbit, Notley Abbey, Buckinghamshire (near Thame).
(d) C 14 tile with spotted butterfly, quadrant $4\frac{1}{2}$ inches square. Midlands design, found at Ashbourne and Morley Churches, Derbyshire.

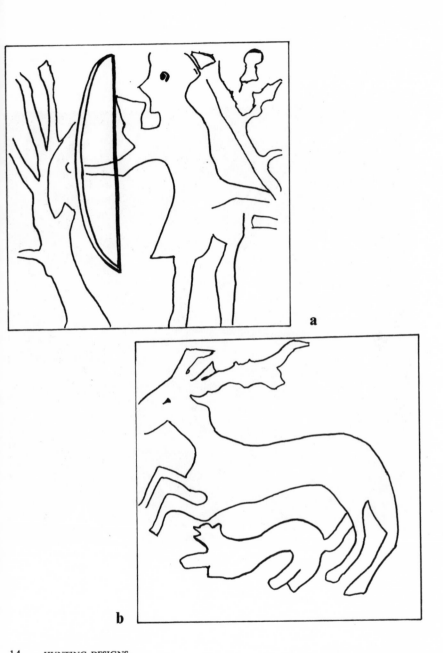

14   HUNTING DESIGNS
(a) Worn tile, 4½ inches square, of bowman in woodland, probably fourteenth-century, in Canterbury Cathedral.
(b) Worn tile. 4½ inches square, of stag and hunting dog, probably fourteenth-century, in Canterbury Cathedral.

15   TRINITY RABBITS

Narrow inlaid design of linked rabbits, symbolising the Holy Trinity, in Chester Cathedral. (About $5\frac{3}{8}$ inches square.)

48

a

b

16   FISH
(a) Fourteenth-century tile at Haccombe Chapel, Devon, with worn design of a
fish and foliage. ($5\frac{1}{2}$ inches square.)
(b) Inlay forming fish.

chemicals were not purified. The addition of copper tended to make the glaze opaque, so relief and other designs may be less clear than designs in the common yellow. Very dark brown or blackish tiles might be achieved by using more copper still, but could also result from low absorption of oxygen by the clay during firing or from over-firing – or a dark-firing clay might have been selected in the first place. Green and dark tiles were most useful for mosaic pavements, but there are some green relief tiles – for example, early ones from All Saints Pavement Church at York, which are now in the Yorkshire Museum there.

The mosaic tiles made by the Cistercians in Yorkshire and west Scotland, from the late twelfth century, had the most varied glazes. Their tilers were able to produce different greens and greys – contemporary with mosaic-style grisaille glass, with near-abstract leaf and vine patterns in grey-green – as well as yellow slip tiles. These colours are still visible *in situ* at Byland and elsewhere, despite wear of the glaze. The Crauden pavement at Ely was mainly brown and yellow, with some green border tiles. Another complex and later mediaeval pavement, of yellow, black (near-black) and green mosaic, has recently been excavated at Norton Priory, Runcorn (Cheshire). Only limited patterns could be set out with two colours of tiles to alternate dark and light; any more elaborate mosaic – such as chains, radiating or fleur-de-lis layouts – needed more colours. The customary details, such as inlaid or line-impressed rosettes, could not provide sufficient differentiation. Thus, even where two colours are dominant, there may be a third auxiliary colour as well as some figured tiles made by a different technique.

The richest yellow glaze seems to have been used only on the inlaid Chertsey and Westminster tiles of the mid-thirteenth century. The peak of achievement reached as early as 1255 in the Westminster Abbey Chapter House tiles owes even more to the exceptional richness of their glaze than to the delicacy of the inlay. The scarcity of other such glazes contributes to a post-Westminster sense of disappointment. In the mid-fifteenth century, though, part of the revival of fine tile-making at Great Malvern Priory was the use of good and varied glazes. These tiles present us with inlays in lilac shades or deep honey, and do not suffer much from competing with the marvellous glass of the same date.

With some exceptions, abrasion of their glaze has long since taken the original glow from the old pavements. In many places we may have to scout round protected corners, such as tomb-bases or recesses or along the risers of steps, to find the full colours of the tile pavement.

After the earlier mosaic tiles the most frequent colouration was the contrast – in the same tile – of the dark ground with the pale inlaid design. The contrast was deepened by the glaze, which usually made the ground a warm reddish brown – rather than the red or pink typical of worn or unglazed tiles. Green, including grey-green, had been regularly employed among the mosaic tiles, but was used much less often for the other types. It was a 'difficult' colour, patchily distributed, but some pavements make one regret that it was not more successful or popular. Meesden Church in Hertfordshire has a fine circular mosaic, made of bright yellow and bright green pieces, which is unrivalled. Its good condition is as uncommon as its colouring. Hailes Church in Gloucestershire has some small inlaid tiles, fairly worn and evidently salvaged from the abbey, which bear heraldic designs done in an unusual muted green, with olive and bluey tones. This green is strangely attractive and in harmonious contrast with the matt brown earthenware ground of the tiles. Surviving green inlays are very rare.

2 THE DIFFERENT TYPES OF DECORATION

Decoration of tiles began here towards the end of the twelfth century, gained strength in the thirteenth century and became common in the fourteenth century. Half a dozen different techniques were employed, sometimes in combination. Even the earliest and purest mosaic tiling, at Rievaulx and Byland abbeys in Yorkshire, included some inlaid flowerets. Two-colour tiles, with inlaid or (later) 'printed' designs, were to gain the final victory in fashion and numbers. Mosaic had been rejected in their favour two centuries before the Dissolution of the Monasteries and seems to have been limited to ecclesiastical buildings. Relief tiles, rejected in their turn, were never widely distributed. Other techniques were not used for whole floors, but for added details or small sections. Tiles from the simplest type of decorated paving, squares of two colours laid alternately either

a

b, c

17   MYTHOLOGICAL CREATURES

(a) Fourteenth-century dark brown relief tile (4 inches square) from Bawsey, Norfolk, found in London and now in the London Museum.

(b) Chertsey and Westminster Abbey Chapter House Basilisk, thirteenth century. Note dragon's head at end of tail.

(c) Wessex Griffin of the thirteenth or fourteenth century.

52

a

b, c

18   MYTHOLOGICAL CREATURES

(a) Dragon with foliate tail on late Wessex inlaid tile in Winchester Cathedral (5 inches square).

(b) Fourteenth-century printed tile of dragon or wyvern. Penn-style tile (5 inches square) found in London.

(c) Fifteenth-century heraldic tile with unicorn (made with cracked stamp) at Bradgate House near Leicester. (About $7\frac{1}{2}$ inches square.)

square or diamond-wise, have not survived well or in quantity. They were the most easily reduced to blank earthenware, since they lacked the pattern of mosaic shape, or any significant identations.

Coloured chequerboard floors of this kind could have been much more common than is suggested by the fragmentary survivals, such as those at Herringfleet. At a guess, they provided a good number of the missing secular floors, for example in the houses of late fourteenth- and early fifteenth-century traders who had achieved prosperity, but had no heraldry. Tiles came late to domestic settings. At the Manor of the More site (Hertfordshire), which was occupied by a series of mediaeval houses, Martin Biddle found from their mortar-beds that the first tiles were laid only about 1426. At this period the manor was held by Henry Beaufort, Bishop of Winchester, whose St. Cross Hospital at Winchester has figured tiles. (See article by Martin Biddle, and others on 'The Excavation of the Manor of the More', in *Archaeological Journal*, CXVI, 1959.) Plain single-colour tiles were also used as a minor element in decorated pavements. Plain dark tiles were quite often used as borders between groups of related inlaid tiles. Additionally, J. B. Ward-Perkins (in the London Museum's *Medieval Catalogue*) noted of plain tiles: 'Used alone they were less common, although in the 15th Century, in East Anglia, large glazed tiles 10 or 11 in. square and coloured brown, yellow, or dark green, enjoyed a considerable popularity ...' Examples were found at Butley Priory, Suffolk, as were small single-colour relief tiles of earlier date.

The different kinds of mediaeval English tiles are described in this *Medieval Catalogue* and in the British Museum *Handbook* by E. Eames. In *A History of Building Materials* (1961) Norman Davey included a chapter on 'Decorative Tiles', which is a good general exposition of these and other types used in different cultures. It is interesting to contrast our insular, weather-confined practices with those of the great architectural users of tiles, the Muslims. The Muslims could employ superb colours, but religious doctrine ensured that the tiles were non-pictorial; a comparatively permissive ideology allowed the mediaeval English tilers to pave even altar platforms both with religious images and, for ornament, with people and hunting dogs and dragons. (Davey, though, cites a non-existent figured pavement in Ely Cathedral.) Contemporary records of tile decoration are included by L. F. Salzman in his *Building in England Down to 1540*, (1952).

What left most trace in the records (usually building accounts) is the most transitory type of decorated tile – tiles with designs painted on with a pale clay slip, as in some pottery decoration. As can be imagined, such designs on floor tiles must have been short-lived and were expensive in labour. Examples are very rare. The British Museum acquired two such tiles from Witham Church in Essex, with a painted flower and a fleur-de-lis (included in the 1903 *Catalogue* by R. L. Hobson), and the Ashmolean at Oxford has a possibly slip-painted fragment from Christ Church College. Mediaeval technical terms can be either vague or misleading, especially during the changeover in documents from Latin to English (fourteenth and fifteenth centuries). English terms are often included in mainly Latin records, but may still not be taken literally. Both Latin *tegula* and English 'tile' (in various spellings) were very general terms, which could also be used for bricks. Some qualification or a clear context is needed if the exact type of tile is to be known, and it rarely is. A 1289 record that 11,500 *de tegulis subtilis* were supplied to Edward I just tells us that these were fine or ingenious and, thus, figured or decorated. By what technique they were decorated is not shown, but they could have been inlaid – like Henry III's pavements. At the start of Edward II's reign, though, the royal accounts recorded that Peter the 'pavier' (paviour) and Hugh the 'peyntour' (painter) were employed for 28 days in 1308 in laying and painting a floor at the Palace of Westminster. In 1385 1,000 tiles called 'pennetyle' were laid at the Palace of Sheen, Richmond (Surrey) and then 2,000 more painted tiles were laid there, in the bathroom of the advanced and fastidious Richard II.

Salzman points out that 'pennetyle' or 'peynt tile', literally painted tiles, was the usual name for decorated tiles. Long predating Malvern Priory's famous inlaid tiles, there is a reference to 'peynt tile' made by the Great Malvern poet of *Piers Plowman* late in the fourteenth century, but he did not necessarily mean tiles with designs painted freehand. On the analogy of the continued mediaeval use of the term 'painted cloths' for the tapestries which replaced them on affluent walls, 'peynt tile' could be conservative usage for any type of coloured or figured tiles. As late as 1482, though, there is an odd definite reference to the painting of tiles – but one that is very difficult to interpret. The accounts of St. George's Chapel in Windsor have an entry for 'divers colours' bought for painting 'paving tile' and locks: the colours were not listed.

(*a*) MOSAIC

The dominant kind of mosaic was introduced by the Cistercian order and apparently last made by them at Meaux in Yorkshire in the mid-thirteenth century. The few other mosaic pavements have much in common with the Cistercian work, though the newly discovered one at Runcorn (Cheshire) has a rougher look. These other pavements take us to the mid-fourteenth century only, when mosaic was evidently abandoned altogether. Some of the early inlaid pavements have mosaic elements, in the sense that they include some simple shapes other than squares, such as rectangles and segments. Some mosaic pieces, seemingly handcut, were found with the relief tile wasters at Bawsey (Norfolk). Likewise, other types of decoration appear on mosaic, but are not essential to it.

The Cistercian style of mosaic was technically very demanding, for fifty or sixty different shapes might be used in a set of pavements at one site. Some were very small. They ranged from obvious forms like rectangles, rhomboids, triangles and circles, to complex polygonal shapes with cusps and lobes. All were difficult to bake successfully. The problems meant that mosaic could never become popular, not even with the religious orders. The layouts – the overall patterns incorporating the pattern shapes – were usually varied rather than complicated, but Newbattle Abbey had its fleur-de-lis layout, and the Benedictine Crauden pavement at Ely is complex. The Crauden pavement also includes unique *irregular* mosaic panels (see Chapter 4, section *c*). Two or three colours were used for mosaic.

In some places the pieces may have been shaped in wood moulds, like the square tiles. Investigation of the Meaux tiles, however, showed that the Cistercian practice was to cut out the shapes. (This is briefly described in the vital article by E. Eames in *Medieval Archaeology*, 1961, published by the Medieval Archaeological Society, c/o University College. Two further, more inaccessible sources are mentioned.) Straight-sided shapes could either be cut out completely or fired in partly-cut blocks that were broken up afterwards – as might also be done with some later square tiles. The shapes that were wholly cut, including all those with curved sides, were each made according to a template. Thick flat blocks of clay were sanded to prevent sticking; workers scored round the templates; the shapes were then cut out and, usually, slightly bevelled to allow a stronger, closer set in their mortar bed. Firing followed a period of natural drying, as with every kind of tile. (See also Chapter 4, *Cistercian and Other Mosaic.*)

(*b*) RELIEF AND COUNTER-RELIEF

Like most mosaic tiles, relief tiles were made in single colours. The scattered distribution of the few surviving examples suggests that there may have been many more, which have been long replaced or had their raised or 'embossed' motifs rubbed away by people's tread. On the other hand their mostly coastal locations suggest that they were an immigrant fashion which did not spread far inland. Most are of the thirteenth century, but they 'enjoyed a considerable local popularity in East Anglia throughout the Middle Ages' – J. B. Ward-Perkins. The late fourteenth-century relief tile kiln at Bawsey (Norfolk), with the many wasters discovered and rediscovered at the site, has been described by E. Eames. Another regional outlier is the seventeenth-century industry which produced the relief tiles found at about thirty places in Devon and Cornwall. This also produced the one old tile design stamp, discovered at Barnstaple in 1900; it bears a fleur-de-lis, which had been the favourite motif among the mediaeval tiles.

Thirteenth-century relief tiles were found at the kiln site at North Berwick (Scotland); the Yorkshire Museum has a fair number, from All Saints Pavement Church in York; the ruined Butley and Leiston Priories in Suffolk retained some examples; Ward-Perkins mentions examples at the Benedictine Priory of Buckfast in South Devon; in the old Cistercian Church of Abbey Dore in Herefordshire there are some very impressive relief tiles, including lozenges with thin foliate fleurs-de-lis in counter-relief; and St. Albans Abbey in Hertfordshire has a few early, rather chunky relief tiles. Those at York are fairly small and of different sizes. They are coloured green or yellow. The displayed examples have geometrical or simple tracery patterns. The Keeper of Archaeology at York says, 'They are thought to be around 1200 but may in fact be earlier'. There are, or were, relief tiles in Ireland, in

St. Patrick's Cathedral and Christ Church Cathedral, Dublin, some similar to Chester tiles (Grosvenor Museum).

The main East Anglian relief tiles belong to the late fourteenth century and to the Bawsey style. They are quite numerous, including many still *in situ* in churches in North Norfolk and the Fenland. The ruined Cluniac Priory at Thetford (Norfolk) has a considerable spread. Slip on the yellow Bawsey tiles is very thin; many are self-coloured only; and they are quite small squares, typical of large production. The numbers of heraldic tiles also indicate a widening and partial secularisation of the market. As many as fifty-seven Bawsey patterns are known, of all types.

Relief, inlaid and printed tiles were usually made square, since this was the most convenient shape. All had designs pressed into the plastic clay with a mould or stamp. For relief tiles this usually carried a countersunk motif, so that the design on the tile was raised. The relief is not normally high, but must still have been uncomfortable underfoot and, inevitably, wore less well than the other types of decorated tiles. Much less often a relief stamp was used, making a counter-relief (*cavo relievo*) pattern on the tiles. Among the wasters at Bawsey were a fair proportion of counter-relief tiles, most with heraldic designs. Among inlaid tiles, however, the occasional counter-relief tiles were probably more often than not accidents – just tiles whose inlay, and therefore second colour, was forgotten. They can only be detected if the glaze remains on the *design* itself; without it, they are almost certainly tiles from which the inlay has chipped out, like the enamel inlay lost from many memorial brasses.

Such a project would have been improbable gimmickry for a mediaeval paviour, yet a floor of countersunk and inlaid versions of just two or three of the same simple designs, with some plain tiles too, could have been attractive.

(*c*) INLAID

The inlaid tiles were the most successful type, and at certain times and places beautiful work was achieved. The employment of two colours – usually yellow on brown – liberated all sorts of artistic possibilities. At the least there was achieved a vivid contrast between dark and light. At the best there were created fine and complex figures. Subtle or detailed designs could be made and *repeated* by

a, b, c

d, e, f

g, h, i

19   FOLIAGE DESIGNS (*not to scale*)
(a) Foliage and keys, Nottingham design. (British Museum.)
(b) Bird and foliage, Cookham-on-Thames Church, Berkshire.
(c) Sycamore scroll, St. Albans Abbey, Hertfordshire.
(d) Acton Burnell Church, Shropshire.
(e) Sandridge Church, Hertfordshire.
(f) Oak leaves, Childrey Church, Berkshire.
(g) Parti-coloured design, C 14, All Saints Church, Leicester.
(h) Mid C 15 design of traceried circle with hawthorn leaves, Great Malvern Priory,
Worcestershire.
(i) 'Dagger' detail from (h).

59

a

20   FLAMBOYANT FOLIAGE DESIGN
(a) Victorian replica, $4\frac{3}{4}$ inches square, of mediaeval tile design at Chastleton Church,
Oxfordshire. (Originals worn, but apparently had more ragged foliage border.)
(b) (c) Mediaeval tiles, approximately 5 inches square, at Bradgate House (chapel)
near Leicester.
(d) FOLIAGE SCROLL: Inlaid tile of about 1325, $4\frac{3}{4}$ inches square, at Clifton House,
King's Lynn, Norfolk.

60

  **b, c**

d

61

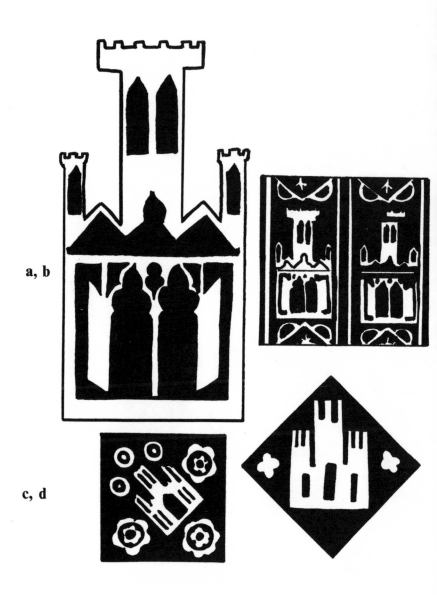

a, b

c, d

21   CASTLES (*not to scale*)
(a) Castle motif from Winchester Cathedral tile (from Gough Nichols' *Examples of Decorative tiles*, 1845).
(b) Thirteenth-century Winchester Cathedral tile, *in situ*.
(c) Thirteenth-century Wessex tile found at Amesbury Abbey, Wiltshire.
(d) Later mediaeval printed tile. (London Museum.)

62

22 RICHARD I ('COEUR DE LION') ON INLAID TILES OF THE LATE THIRTEENTH CENTURY

Chertsey Roundel (diameter about 11 inches). British Museum

Wessex tile $(9\frac{1}{2} \times 6\frac{1}{2}$ inches).
Cleeve Abbey, Somerset

KNIGHT ON HORSEBACK
Victorian copy of mediaeval design ($4\frac{1}{4}$ inches square), in antechamber of Westminster Abbey Chapter House.

63

this method only. Inlaid designs also wore the best, for the pale slip inlay was flush with the tile ground.

Some minor inlays had been used with mosaic, but inlaid pavements were introduced south of the Thames and in the thirteenth century. They were introduced in the royal palaces of Henry III and at important monastic sites like Romsey in Hampshire and Salisbury in Wiltshire. They were followed by the laying of related tiles at other Wiltshire sites and also in Dorset and Somerset. Theirs has been labelled the 'Wessex' style. Perhaps the most important type of design they introduced was heraldry. They also introduced, or certainly popularised, the fleur-de-lis – the 'heraldry' of the Virgin Mary – which became overwhelmingly the favourite tile motif of the Middle Ages. Production of inlaid tiles in the Wessex region itself continued right into the sixteenth century: quality stayed comparatively high, but the later designs are often smaller and simpler versions of the earlier ones. Production of inlaid tiles in other areas was more spasmodic and inconsistent, but Wessex did not have the monopoly of fine work. The inlay technique was evidently French in origin. But as with memorial brasses and the Perpendicular development of Gothic architecture the insular pupils diverged from Continental practices and attained a special and original excellence. The fifteenth-century inlaid tiles of Great Malvern, for example, are unrivalled abroad.

The first stage of putting the pattern on the tile was the same as for relief and line-impressed tiles – that is to press the design into the clay with a carved wooden stamp. No mediaeval stamp, nor apparently even a picture of one, has survived. A modern one now in Winchester City Museum may be a fair representation. It is probably Victorian, perhaps made when new tiles of mediaeval design were being produced for the Cathedral. The design is deeply cut on a flat block and there is a thick rounded handle, similar to, but necessarily much heftier than, a buttermould's. Possibly it was a model, to be followed by later mechanical production.

The stamp would have been cut deeper than the final inlay, allowing for the shrinkage of up to a third overall in firing. The impression would be filled up with clay slip when the ground clay was rather less tacky – so that the surplus could be scraped off cleanly. The early Wessex tiles and others were deeply inlaid. Sometimes they have a quarter of an inch of slip. Good shallower inlays, such as the fourteenth-century Midlands designs, may be about a tenth of an inch deep. Careful inlaid work could achieve very fine lines, such as the foliage scrolls and precise mythological creatures typical of Wessex, and also such difficult motifs as alphabets, religious monograms and other longer inscriptions. For inscriptions the letters of the stamp needed to be cut in reverse, though this was sometimes forgotten. The inlaid tiles are characterised by their distinct outlines. Figures and many patterns were most effectively presented in this way.

(d) PRINTED OR STAMPED

The technique for making the tiles now known as 'printed' or 'stamped' was a clumsy version of inlaying. It speeded the rate of production by saving workers' time, and prompted or allowed a more commercialised distribution of stock items. With some notable exceptions – which were always inlaid tiles – the fall-off in the quality of the later polychrome tiles disappoints modern researchers. It was evidently also disappointing to those important mediaeval buyers who avoided it by commissioning new designs for inlaying, including their own coats-of-arms and badges, or who imported decorated tiles from north Europe. The technique, a kind of hand-printing, was detected by Loyd Haberly, whose main study was of the Penn-type Buckinghamshire and Oxfordshire tiles. (See Booklist.) Following his observations, he experimented with making printed tiles. Norman Davey describes the method severely as 'an alternative and slovenly method which became general in the Thames Basin in the middle of the fourteenth century'. It was suggested to Haberly by the economical shallowness of their pipeclay and by the frequent blurring of designs that the design stamps themselves were coated with slip, so that outline and colour were added in one operation.

The general tendencies of printing can be detected, even though it may not be easy to classify particular tiles as printed rather than inlaid. The stock tiles are comparatively small, about four-and-a-half inches square, and have no keys. The same kinds of designs as for inlaid tiles were often used but in simplified and cut-down versions that were cut less deeply on the stamps. The results are bald fattish patterns with unsharp edges. A thin layer of slip was spread on the design stamp and impressed on the ground clay. The outlines were often smeared when the stamp was removed, especially if too much slip was used, in strong contrast to the deep and narrow inlays of

a, b, c

d, e, f

g, h, i

23　HERALDRY ON TILES (*not to scale*)

(a) Diamond chequer or 'lozengy'. C 14 Bawsey relief tile (single colour), Castle Rising (Castle), Norfolk.

(b) Three 'chevronels' of Clare family. C 14 Bawsey relief tile, Castle Rising and Thetford Cluniac Priory, Norfolk.

(c) Three 'bendlets' of Branscombe. C 14 inlaid tile, Haccombe Chapel, Devon.

(d) 'Vair' design (two-colour furs). C 14 printed tile, St. Bartholomew's Priory Church, Smithfield, London.

(e) 'Botonné' crosses of Beauchamp of Warwick. C 14 inlaid tile, Bradgate House (chapel), near Leicester.

(f) Covered cups of Boteler (Butler). C 14 inlaid tile, Chastleton Church, Oxfordshire.

(g) Triple heraldic tile. C 14 Penn-style printed tile, London Museum.

(h) 'Cross crosslets' of Berkeley of Berkeley Castle, Gloucestershire. Later mediaeval inlaid tile found at Reading Abbey, Berkshire.

(i) 'Fretty' (interlace) arms of Despenser. C 14 inlaid tile, Croxton Abbey, Leicestershire.

66

a, b, c

d, e, f

24   HERALDIC ANIMALS ON INLAID TILES (*not to scale*)

(a) Double-headed or Imperial eagle of Richard Earl of Cornwall as King of the Romans. Late C 13, Cleeve Abbey, Somerset.

(b) Double-headed eagle. C 14, Haccombe Chapel, Devon.

(c) Double-headed eagle, with fleur-de-lis tail. C 14, St. Mary de Castro Church, Leicester.

(d) Royal swan badge. C 15, Great Malvern Priory, Worcestershire.

(e) Shield with three hedgehogs. C 14, St. Mary de Castro Church, Leicester.

(f) Inscribed tile with talbot dog, badge of Sir John Talbot, The lettering is inlaid. About 1460, Canynges pavement (Bristol), now in British Museum.

25   HERALDIC EAGLE
Early sixteenth-century parti-coloured tile design, $5\frac{7}{8}$ inches square, recorded at
Hailes Abbey in Gloucestershire and published by Gough Nichols in 1845. Examples
of this design, which was probably inspired by a thirteenth-century original, have
survived at Southam de la Bere, Gloucestershire.

68

26   ECCLESIASTICAL HERALDRY

(a) Tile design of mitre and arms of John Carpenter, Bishop of Worcester 1443–1476. 4½ inches square. (Worcester Cathedral.)

(b) Heraldically correct version of arms of Carpenter.

(c) Mid fifteenth-century tile design from Great Malvern Priory, Worcestershire, with mitre and rebus of Tydeman de Winchcomb, Bishop of Worcester (1395–1401): a rope is wound or *tied* round a *winch* (capstan), with a wool comb above. (*Not to scale*) Both tiles were reproduced in Gough Nichols' *Examples of Decorative Tiles* (1845): the originals are now lost.

69

Wessex. The resulting pseudo-inlay was too shallow to wear as well, yet many survive.

There is a modish league-table which gives so much attention to the rating of technical competence in tiles five hundred years old or more that their subjects are virtually ignored, except as a means of detecting their area of origin. Also ignored is their meaning for the people who first ordered and trod on them. The league-table puts these printed tiles at the bottom, yet their very mass-production is interesting because it evinces the popularisation of decorated tiles. It was this technique that brought them in demonstrably large quantities, and with pleasing if comparatively unsubtle effect, to numerous country churches north and north-west of London. They put roses and rabbits and dragons on the floor, for pewless and bookless peasants to observe.

(e) LINE-IMPRESSED, INCISED AND SGRAFFITO

Line-impressed tiles were decorated by the use of stamps bearing exceptionally thin carved forms. Incised and *sgraffito* tiles were decorated freehand. None of these methods made deep markings on the tiles, and so designs made in this way have not usually worn well. None were used, it seems, for complete floors; they were used for small groups of tiles or to supplement mosaic or inlays. The freehand techniques were obviously not suitable for large-scale production.

The line-impressed tiles have such thin lines that they used to be described as incised, but comparisons of a few tiles with the same pattern will reveal their perfect regularity. The stamps must have been remarkably well carved, but in low relief for the designs do not go deep into the tiles. They are not, therefore, clear from any distance in either self-colour or single-colour slip tiles. They were used mostly with mosaic. J. B. Ward-Perkins noted (in the London Museum Catalogue) that they were used only in the fourteenth century, and that distribution was almost limited to Shropshire, Cheshire, Staffordshire and parts of East Anglia, including the Fenland. There are other scattered examples, such as those found at Elstow in Bedfordshire, where there was a Benedictine nunnery. The most typical design, perhaps, is the double or triple round-petalled rosette which is used on the major pavements at Meesden (Hertfordshire) and Ely. The pavement found at Runcorn in Cheshire includes line-impressed trefoils, set in the centre of mosaic flowers. At Runcorn, too, and at Icklingham All Saints' Church in Suffolk are square tiles with larger linear designs, such as faces, foliage, pinnacles and pairs of birds. The simple repeated rosettes, two inches across, remind one a little of the cinquefoil flowers that were often stencilled on church walls and on painted screens.

Incised tiles were made by scoring the design freehand in the damp clay with some sharp tool. As with the line-impressed tiles, the glaze would later run down into the hollows. A type of decoration that was distinct on pottery was necessarily less clear down on the floor. The technique, though, was particularly suitable for small special orders, and there may have been many more such tiles than the few survivors suggest. Hitchin Church in Hertfordshire has one mediaeval tile, incised with the figure of a fourteenth-century layman: this cannot have been unique. There were probably also more tiles with incised inscriptions, such as simple dedications or memorials. To score the words in clay for baking would have been easier and cheaper than carving in brass, stone or even wood. The large relief tiles that make up two early sixteenth-century tombs at Lingfield Church in Surrey include incised inscriptions. Another use of incision was to add details to inlaid tiles or to sharpen part of their outlines. This was done after the design had been pressed into the plastic clay and before the addition of the clay slip. Significant examples are the little star added on the cross-bar in the Boteler arms (of salt-cellars) at Chastleton Church (Oxfordshire) and the incised points of a sunburst design at Tewkesbury Abbey (Gloucestershire). (The sunburst is on a damaged tile in a recess on the south side of the abbey.) Contrariwise, a very rough sunburst design found at Bradgate House in Leicestershire was not drawn freehand, but was the product of a badly cut stamp. (See N. Whitcomb, *The Mediaeval Floor-Tiles of Leicestershire*.) The Chastleton sun was a special extra marking, an heraldic cadency sign, used for a junior member of the family.

Sgraffito tiles were also incised freehand, but the design was drawn and scraped into a wet slip coating. Cipriano Piccolpasso in the sixteenth century called this *sgraffiato*, and the term is derived from *sgraffiare*, the Italian verb 'to scratch'. (Another obvious relation is *graffiti*.) There are various spellings, but no English version because the technique was not common here. The *sgraffito* method was also occasionally used for pottery decoration. The ground would be left

71

bare, so that pale figures stood out against a dark ground, while all the details of the figures were also dark or darkish. Since the slip was raised, this technique was really even more extravagant for floors than the lost painted tiles. Examples are rare, though S. E. Rigold mentions 'early *graffiti* type tiles (found) at Faversham', Kent.

There are just two sets of notable *sgraffito* tiles, of quite different types, but both of the early fourteenth century. The Crauden pavement at Ely, which happily illustrates most techniques, includes some *sgraffito* work, now very worn, in the slip-coated irregular mosaic of large lions and in the 'Temptation' scene. Such details as hair and leaf-veining have been added in this way. The other set of tiles is unique and highly individualistic, although related to the Chertsey tiles and bearing designs inspired by an illuminated manuscript. These are the wall-tiles of the 'Apocryphal Infancy of Christ', which once belonged to Tring Church in Hertfordshire. The set is incomplete, but in good condition and richly-glazed.

The 'Apocryphal Infancy' tiles have a rare vividness. They have attracted much attention, but are an aside for us since they belonged to a narrative wall-frieze – like a religious strip cartoon – and now have no fellows. To ignore them, however, would be something like inverted snobbery, and their subject matter is anyway a stark and useful warning against sloppy, anachronistic thinking. Eight of the tiles are in the British Museum and two, with some fragments, in the Victoria and Albert Museum. The eight were bought in the 1840s from a 'curiosity shop' in Tring by the Rev. Edward Owen, and some fragments were found when a flint wall at the church was demolished in the 1870s. The tiles were probably first taken from the church after the Reformation, and then dispersed again during Victorian restoration. There is no way of telling how many there were originally or if there were similar sets elsewhere, but Tring was not an important place and even lacked a priory or other religious house.

A complete tile measures about twelve by seven inches, but a vertical bar of slip divides each into two scenes. Fifteen scenes survive, including one of Jesus blessing a family feast and this one covers the whole tile. M. R. James showed how they were probably inspired by an early fourteenth-century French manuscript in the Bodleian Library at Oxford (MS Selden 38). They are not exact copies. The manuscript stories belong to the mediaeval *Liber de Infantia* tradition (the *Book of the Childhood* of Christ), based on a Latin so-called

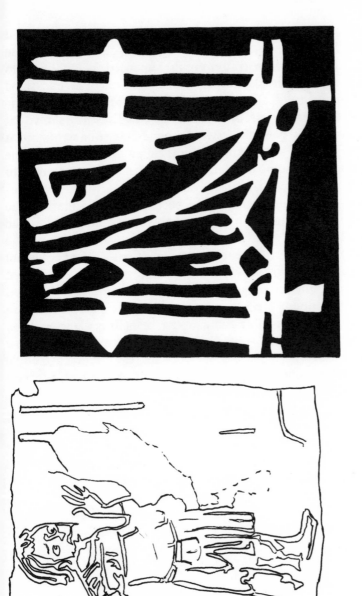

HALF-FIGURE
Inlaid tile, 6¾ inches square, from Reading Abbey, Berkshire.

27   INCISED TILE
Present state of a mid fourteenth-century incised tile, bearing the figure of a layman, in Hitchin Church, Hertfordshire. 5½ inches square'.

Gospel of St. Thomas. These stories filled in with invention the period of Christ's life omitted from the Gospels. The Bodleian manuscript has fifty-six illustrations of the supposed acts of the Child Jesus as apprentice miracle-worker. Some were pleasant and some were horrifyingly brutal, although the brutal ones were reversed by the Child after the complaints of those involved. The tiles show, for example, a wonderful corn harvest and the stretching of a wrongly-cut timber for a plough, but in another miracle an aggressive boy falls dead and in another some children are turned into pigs – in order to punish their parents for disrespect.

Scratched Roman numbers on the back of the tiles marked the correct order for setting in the wall, probably round the chancel. The frieze was a once-off commission, each scene being a strong and individual 'drawing' in the wet clay. The emotions of the people are clear from their posture as well as by expressions and emphatic gestures. The Child achieves his effects with smugness. Robes and tunics, hats and hoods are firmly outlined. People's clothes are full of folds. The figures look like some on the formalistic Chertsey tiles, but have been driven into action by a skilled caricaturist. This man knew well, or was also involved in drawing, the irreverent people and creatures who commandeered the margins of rich men's service books. The clay was only superficially a simpler medium.

CHAPTER FOUR

Cistercian and other mosaic

(a) CLASSIC CISTERCIAN

The abstract mosaic that we can regard as classic belongs, in the main, to the north and to the earliest English and Scottish houses of the Cistercian order. These were isolated foundations of the kind that would be mourned by Robert Aske, leader of the Pilgrimage of Grace of 1536: 'divers and many of the said abbeys were in the mountains and desert places where the people are rude of condition and not well taught the law of God'. Their hospitality and their industry were particularly vital in the sparsely developed terrain of Yorkshire. At least until the Black Death of 1349 Rievaulx Abbey provided jobs and a home for *hundreds* of lay workmen at a time, including wool workers. The mosaic belongs to the twelfth and the early thirteenth century, but it was still being made between 1249 and 1269 at Meaux Abbey (Wawne) in the East Riding.

The Cistercian order had been initiated at Clairvaux in France in 1098, to live by a remodelled and sterner Benedictine rule. When Bernard of Clairvaux died in 1153, the new leadership was prepared to build and furnish grandly, expressing the 'power and prestige' (Andrew Martindale) which the order had gained. (See also Chapter 1.) This material programme was followed against internal opposition and was typified by the erection of a new church at Clairvaux itself. Major Cistercian buildings were made elsewhere in France, the scale of which we can best see in the ruins of Fountains Abbey in the West Riding. The conflict in the order was like that among the Franciscans two hundred years later, when the 'Spiritual Franciscans' broke away from the embarrassingly rich parent body. In this country, though, members of the Cistercian order – unlike the Benedictines or the Augustinian canons – never ran great churches and cathedrals in important centres of population. The rural isolation of their monasteries has aided the survival of tiles *in situ* for rediscovery, but also made them vulnerable to eighteenth- and nineteenth-century landlords of landscaping, agricultural or even antiquarian persuasion.

The geometrical mosaic that had been developed in France was made and laid in the first houses here about the end of the twelfth century, but the technique was abandoned in the thirteenth century. Despite St. Bernard's injunctions against both elaborate building and pictorial art, Cistercians here became also key patrons of decorated tiling – even of heraldic designs. When Meaux was still making mosaic, inlaid or figured tiling was already established in Cistercian monasteries in the south, as well as at other ecclesiastical and some royal sites. They have left us examples of inlaid tiles in many places, even as far from the original centres as the West Country, Worcestershire and Wales.

In the classic style the figurative element had been slight, but the variety of shapes was great. Between the late kiln site of Meaux and its lost church the tiles remaining and the marks in the empty mortar beds added up to fifty different shapes. As many had been used at the turn of the twelfth century at Byland, where the greatest amount remains *in situ* still.

Even at the beginning many of the shapes were far from new: it is not just the alternation of dark and light but many of the specific patterns that take us back to classical Greek and Roman mosaic. The radiating design of rectangles and octagons, for instance, which is used at Byland and Rievaulx is literally classical. It contributes one panel to a marvellous example of Roman mosaic found at Nîmes in Provence (*Mosaique dite du Mariage d' Admète, Musée des Beaux Arts*). Some of the less geometrical forms only, like Byland's 'toy guardsmen' (or nine-pins) or the curved octagonal 'cowhide' shape (like the 'real leather' symbol), lack clear classical inspiration. Even so, they are still coolly precise, a stylish remove away from much contemporary mediaeval art or craft, whether vivid or clumsy.

Besides the essential material differences between the squared marble chips used for tessellated classical mosaic and the variety of heavy clay shapes, there are other differences. Various classical elements are missing from our classic Cistercian pavings. Not only

76

are the pictures and foliage scrolls absent, but so are the more linear classical patterns – keys, swastika, egg-and-dart, acanthus derivations, the twisted guilloche. The colouring of the clay pieces was less complex that that of most classical mosaic, and for technical reasons the colour contrasts were muted – and have been further muted, of course, by wear. As one result, although we do get simple shifts or reversals of ground and abstract 'object' between these comparatively large dark and light pieces, the subtle *trompe l'oeil* and flickering kinetic effects are absent. Such illusionary effects had been achieved with three or four colours of tesserae, a favourite kind being the panels of 'three-dimensional' steps. A second-century example from Antioch is illustrated in E. H. Gombrich's *Art and Illusion* (1960), its steps formed hexagonally like the volcanic lava steps of the Giant's Causeway, County Antrim. The Cistercians' greys – and sometimes black – greens and yellow slip-coated tiles were a gentler medium, despite the high demands of their shaping and firing. (See Chapter 3, section 2*a*.) The permutations were obtained less by ingeniously-achieved spontaneous alternations of perception than by the multiplication of forms.

Sixty or seventy different shapes are known, shared – like the layouts – between several sites. The closest correspondence is perhaps between Byland, Rievaulx (including the British Museum tiles) and Melrose Abbey in Scotland. These places have the dominant green or grey and yellow colouring. Fountains Abbey had black with yellow. At Revesby in Lincolnshire the colours are green and light brown, with some black. A few brown tiles were found at Meaux. As the experts have pointed out, it is the glazes and the body clay that vary from site to site, but a number of mobile craftsmen certainly shared methods and technical expertise, templates and patterns between the sites. The bulk of the shapes are straight-sided – the obvious ones, and wedges, diamonds, stars and triangular *gyronny* (as at Newbattle) – certainly because these responded more reliably to firing. All the same, as well as layouts like the thirteenth-century fleur-de-lis 'of considerable complexity' found at Newbattle, there are many curved and polygonal shapes. One curvilinear pattern that is both particularly attractive and complex is the double chain or 'chain-belt' pattern found at Byland and also still *in situ* at Rievaulx: this consists of big slip-coated curved and cross-barred 'Xs' set in a ground made of dark hollow lozenges and twin-lobed shapes. Each

28   Thirteenth-century mosaic tiles at Rievaulx Abbey, Yorkshire. (*Not to scale*).

'X' has a total of fourteen sides and blunted ends! Even the simpler 'cowhide' shape has ten unequal and concave sides, while Rievaulx's cusped quatrefoils – set out alternately in dark and light versions – made at least as niggling demands on jointing. Fountains Abbey, which was founded in the same year (1132), retains rather more curvilinear forms than the pillaged Rievaulx, which was the first English house of the order.

The eventual retreat from this genuinely interlocking type of mosaic is perfectly comprehensible: there was no chance of its popularisation. Significantly, even Jervaulx Abbey in the North Riding, also founded in 1132 – nearly half-a-century before Byland (1177) – chose Wessex-style inlaid mosaic, with its uncomplicated rectangular and off-square pieces. We can find mosaic in this country from the turn of the twelfth century at Byland to the mid-fourteenth century, but the classic and elaborate geometry did not last long. There is consistency and even duplication between the earlier mosaic of

Rievaulx, Byland, Fountains, Newbattle, Melrose and the last batch, produced between 1249 and 1269 (the dates of the ninth abbot) for the church at Meaux; beyond the remote main sites the curved polygonal forms declined in number and complexity, and this was increasingly compensated for by the addition of inlaid or line-impressed decoration to the pieces. These main sites are state-administered and their surviving mosaic is looked after, even though the official guidebooks pay it disappointingly slight attention. A detailed and illustrated study of mosaic in Scotland was, however, included in the 1928/9 article by Richardson (see Booklist).

There are scantier relics at other places, which may be interpreted with knowledge gained from the main sites and from the 1957 Meaux kiln excavation. This applies to Newminster Abbey in Northumberland, which was founded in 1138 from Fountains, and to Sawley Abbey in the West Riding, which was founded in 1148 from Newminster: both retain fragmentary mosaic paving. From sites where the remains of buildings above ground are comparatively small the tiles have usually been dispersed to private collections and to museums. This has happened at Meaux from the 1920s and 1930s on, when part of the kiln at North Grange was first located and the site of the abbey church was excavated (see Eames article in Booklist). Notable thirteenth-century tiles from Newbattle Abbey at Dalkeith in Midlothian were transferred to the site museum at Melrose Abbey (Roxburgh) and to the national museums in Edinburgh. Melrose itself has only patches of mosaic *in situ*, but the museum in the Commendator's House has more mosaic and also square inlaid tiles of later date. The mosaic incorporates some rare two-colour slip decoration, besides stamped motifs.

If we turn to southern England the traces of classic mosaic range from the incoherent to the impressive, but all are tantalising in different ways. The site of Revesby Abbey in Lincolnshire (Lindsey), which was founded in 1142 from Rievaulx, is empty of buildings, but long panels of fine thirteenth-century mosaic were once uncovered on the site of the nave, when *ten* different layouts were recorded. Revesby parish church, which dates from 1891, has a section of 'about $4\frac{1}{2}$ by 6 ft' from one panel, with 'a complicated pattern of large six-pointed stars'. The colours are green and dull brown, with some black. (Source: Norma Whitcomb, quoted in *Lincolnshire* by Nikolaus Pevsner and John Harris, 1964). Much more fragmentary and mixed remains were salvaged from the bare site of Sawtry Abbey in Huntingdonshire and were set in a two-foot square frame in the parish church, an 1880 rebuilding. Sawtry Abbey was set up in 1147 from Warden Abbey in Bedfordshire, itself founded as a daughter house of Fountains in 1136. There are thirty-four tiles plus fragments, incidentally the county's only mediaeval tiles. They are worn relics of thirteenth- and fourteenth-century floors of different types and even of different clays (pink and buff). There are: mosaic tiles; worn inlaid tiles, including fleur-de-lis and dragon designs; one relief tile, its design 'like a large piece out of the crust of a pork pie'. The mosaic tiles are glazed black, dark green and olive. They are straight-sided only: a triangle, squares and 'truncated wedges', these with sides six inches long and the ends three-and-a-half and two inches. Most interestingly, and making a link with fourteenth-century mosaic at Meesden, Runcorn and Ely, there are small line-impressed 'flowers' with circular petals (of two different designs). One of these motifs rather surprisingly appears on a black tile. (Source: detailed information in a letter from the Rev. T. H. W. Swan.)

At Old Warden the site of Warden Abbey is marked by just one ruined monastic building, which was converted into a house soon after the Dissolution. The monastery was founded by Walter Espec a few years after Rievaulx and was developed into a particularly large complex. In Victorian times the site was partly excavated and recorded by Bradford Rudge, a schoolmaster and artist from Bedford. In the early 1960s it was re-excavated by the Bedford Archaeological Society, with Tom Rudd as director. Until this date only fragments of thirteenth-century mosaic tiling were known, so the discovery of 'an extensive area' of mosaic on the site of the church (? south transept) was exciting. It was deeply dented, evidently by the fall of stonework after the Dissolution. Despite this and the wear suffered by the glaze, the tiles were well-preserved. (See Joyce Godber, *History of Bedfordshire*, published by the County Council in 1969.) Records were made and examples removed, but the pavement was left again tantalisingly invisible – under protecting layers of sand, soil and turf. What impressed the excavators was the elaborate, careful interlocking of many different shapes 'dovetailed' to form 'a magnificent large-scale pattern'. There were simple shapes, such as adjacent circles and hollow diamonds, and complex shapes like the curling serrated 'petals' that formed large flower heads. There were also small tiles line-impressed with stars, compass-drawn flowers and fleurs-de-lis with rosettes. These extra motifs are a development of work at Byland, which has its few *inlaid* six-petalled flowers (round the circular panel), and are also precursors of the less complicated but more decorated later mosaic.

It is not surprising that the Meaux abbey site is bare, for the church was demolished as early as 1542 and the materials used for Henry VIII's new harbour fortifications at Kingston-upon-Hull. Yet enough of the late but still classic mosaic has been found in this century to establish that Meaux had the usual panels of different shapes, the simple as well as the most difficult geometry of polygonal forms, done mostly in yellow and dark green. We can also see, however, the increase in the figure shapes. Besides the 'chain' or curved X pattern (*in situ* at Rievaulx and Byland), which only arguably belongs to this non-abstract category, there are mosaic fleurs-de-lis, rounded arcading and columns and pairs of slim birds set back-to-back and in profile – like the popular Wessex design. For the rest of the Middle Ages such designs were made more easily, but in a single and so more monotonous colour scheme, with stamps and slip inlays. Rievaulx itself has in the ruined nave a large number of square fourteenth-century inlaid tiles, mostly with fleur-de-lis and foliage patterns – though a few are also inscribed and there is a rectangular tile with a small griffin and a double-headed eagle.

The mosaic of Rievaulx and Byland may be considered together. There is no substitute for visiting these two sites in Yorkshire's North Riding. They are only four miles apart. The British Museum, though, has a large part of the north transept floor from Byland and still more mosaic from Rievaulx (all long stored in cardboard boxes), 'lifted' by Rutland. Byland had the largest Cistercian church in England, 330 ft. long and 140 ft. across the transepts. This great church was once 'amost entirely' paved with yellow and green mosaic, with some grey pieces too. It still has the largest amount *in situ*, the bulk of it in the two south transept chapels. Rievaulx has mosaic of exactly the same kind in the superb Early English ruins. Patches survive in the nave, which was 170 ft. long, in the choir and the presbytery (the eastern section of the church) and in a south transept chapel. Rievaulx was founded in 1132 by Walter Espec, lord of nearby Helmsley, and Byland was founded in 1177 by the survivors or successors of the monks who had left Furness Abbey in 1134. The church was begun immediately after they had settled finally at Byland, and this work probably stimulated the whole Cistercian tile-making industry: 'at Byland are late C 12 and early C 13 tiled floors as good as any in England' (Pevsner). Although the kiln, or its ground plan, has not survived at Byland, its presence is proved by the find of a 'mass of fused wasters'. While the dark colours at the abbeys have mainly been reduced to earthenware, the contrast is maintained through the survival of the cream slip of the yellow tiles. The coated tiles were used in smaller numbers, so 'dark' is now dominant.

In both places some of the most important sections of mosaic, and naturally the least worn, are the narrow bands set along the risers of low steps. Most of these bands consist of two or three shapes only: dark and light squares, diamonds, equilateral and isosceles triangles, various 'ninepin' forms with rounded or oval heads and their matching polygonal 'grounds'. Similar strips of mosaic are used for the borders or edging strips between the main panels. It is interesting to see the different effects achieved when the same pieces are used for narrow bands instead of larger blocks, which may necessitate rearranging or dissecting them. The curved X pattern loses its chain effect when the complete Xs are set out in a single row on top of each other, instead of side by side. When it is halved to line a step riser it looks like a tiny and complex ogee arcade (without the piers).

More complete layouts have survived at Byland than at Rievaulx, with a higher proportion of really green tiles. We see square and rectangular panels, of varying widths, with slight relation between adjacent panels – though a border strip may pick up one or two elements of a panel. Most panels are strictly geometrical, composed of straight-sided but versatile pieces, especially diamonds, and the simpler curved shapes. These shapes are used in several different ways. There are fewer of the multi-curved patterns, which use quatrefoils, pinched ovals, segments of circles and other polygonal shapes. One unelaborate layout centres on an eight-petalled flower. The four-petalled stylised flowers made of curved triangles take us back to Roman mosaic, such as the triple versions at Woodchester in Gloucestershire (the pavement uncovered in 1963 and 1973), though their 'broken' circular borders foreshadow Ely's side panels. The curved chain and 'bull's-eye' panels foreshadow Ely's centre panel and are also made with five shapes – but simpler ones. The small size of most of the older mosaic shapes is perhaps surprising: a circle only

BYLAND ABBEY, YORKSHIRE Yellow, green and grey mosaic paving of later twelfth century or early thirteenth century *in situ* in remains of south transept of Cistercian abbey.

83

two-and-three-quarter inches in diameter, for example, may even be halved when needed at the edge of a panel. The only panel that uses irregular shapes is the most striking one, the big circular pattern set out in front of a stone altar in Byland's south transept – but which is known from other places too. Surrounding a flower of sixteen rounded petals are bands of diamonds and compass-made flowers or windmills. The main circle and the small circles in the spandrels of the panel are framed plainly with irregular straight-edged pieces.

In total, dark tiles cover a bigger area, but the light tiles set going any mobile effects. These effects are strongest in panels made up of the simpler shapes, even just of dark and light squares and triangles. A panel of skewed oblongs, with sides three by one-and-a-half inches, and three-inch squares switches between making parti-coloured pointed crosses, six-pointed stars and framed diamonds. The precise radiating pattern of pale rectangles and dark triangles and octagons, which is literally classical, if observed at an angle breaks up into diagonal stripes and zigzags. In a panel of three small shapes (dark triangles and slip-coated squares and narrow lozenges) the dominant shape moves between wide-ended crosses, four-pointed stars, concave diamonds, pointed ovals, hexagons, large circles – or, strictly, twelve-sided polygons – and other forms.

However reverent may have been the care that went into the making of these ingenious dovetailing shapes, they could have constituted a hypnotic distraction from prayer – surely even more potent than the comparatively naïve figures and designs that were to become popular? That these reactions are not over-imaginative or exaggerated is suggested, if not proved, by their coming in response even to the 'shade' of the original paving and with the realisation that the impact must have been greater on the freer minds of people who had much, much less to look at each day. This vivid mosaic may seem to us a happy and technically accomplished departure from the waste of certain energies entailed in plain austerity. Despite Bernard of Clairvaux's views, it is just because it is non-didactic – without images, pictures or symbols, even – that we see a kind of luxury in this paving.

(*b*) THE RUNCORN DEVELOPMENT AND MOSAIC IN EASTERN ENGLAND

One can reasonably group the other important mosaic floors (or remains of floors) in a class headed by the great worn pavement in

I   CLEEVE ABBEY, SOMERSET   Later thirteenth-century
Wessex-style inlaid tiles, part of the old refectory floor at the Cistercian
abbey, with the lion arms of Richard of Cornwall and the three
chevrons of Clare.

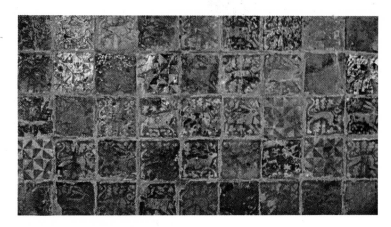

II GREYFRIARS CHURCH
READING, BERKSHIRE Small
fourteenth-century Penn-style tiles
with worn slip designs (re-set in
concrete and framed). *Top*: Complete
panel of 45 tiles. *Left*: *Gyronny*, with
unusual detached triangles. *Below
left*: Dog, hare, *gyronny*. *Below right*:
Dog, stag.

III   *Top* CANYNGES PAVEMENT, FROM BRISTOL Sixteen-tile groups from pavement now in the British Museum, with inlaid designs of heraldic shields and dragons (worn), foliage, flowers, vine leaves and grapes. *Bottom* WESTMINSTER ABBEY CHAPTER HOUSE Inlaid Chertsey-style tiles of 1253–1259, with design of cock and fox.

IV   GREAT
MALVERN PRIORY,
WORCESTERSHIRE
Six-inch square finely inlaid
tiles of the mid-fifteenth century, in Benedictine Priory
church.

Royal arms, the three lions
of England.

Family arms, including the
shield of the Braci family of
Madresfield (with two spur
rowels).

Black Letter inscription: the
prayer or dedication opening
mentem sanctam (a holy
mind).

Complex rose window
design

Prior Crauden's Chapel at Ely, in the Fenland. This chapel was erected in the 1320s among the living and working quarters of the Benedictine monastery, south of the cathedral. In this group of two- or three-colour mosaics much extra decoration was supplied by line-impressed motifs, very susceptible to wear because of their fineness, which was perhaps achieved by metal rather than wood stamps. To the group can now be attached the surprising pavement excavated in 1971 at the site of Norton Priory at Runcorn, Cheshire. Although this includes forms unmatched elsewhere and has the colour black uniquely dominant, it shares with Ely certain shapes and impressed motifs. Other sites beyond East Anglia where similar thin stamped designs have been found are Elstow Nunnery in Bedfordshire (supplemented by recent new excavations) and Pipewell Abbey in Northamptonshire (finds in the British Museum). In the nineteenth century tiles at Higham Ferrers Church in Northamptonshire were compared with the Crauden pavement, but the fourteenth-century tiles surviving there are much less ambitious than Ely's: these are black and yellow square tiles, scored evenly with smaller squares and bearing some line-impressed rosettes.

The mosaic shapes of the Crauden group and of Runcorn are not isolated either from traditional Cistercian mosaic or from some inlaid designing. After all, the abstract or geometrical shape was itself the design and there was a limit to the convenient or practical shapes available. The main elements of Ely's regular mosaic, the plain and the twisted chains made of circles and curved bands, were preceded by more simply composed chains at Byland and Rievaulx. Some geometrical inlays were mosaic-inspired, condensing the dark and light pieces onto one tile – like the triangular *gyronny*, for example. Where Ely and Runcorn have yellow six-pointed stars alternating with dark hexagons, the ordinary inlaid design would be a pale star set in its own dark ground. Quadrants, though, are closer to mosaic technique. We may, for example, compare Runcorn's stars with early Wessex inlaid ones in Winchester Cathedral. Runcorn (but not Ely) has stars made – rather as the indented arms of a Maltese cross – of six 'V' shapes; Winchester has panels of four-pointed stars, made of four tiles each inlaid with a 'V'.

The site of Norton Priory, an Augustinian foundation – with little known history, but unpopularly suppressed with the lesser monasteries in 1536 – is now included in parkland for Runcorn New

85

G

Town. The 1971 excavation was led by J. Patrick Greene, Field Archaeologist for Runcorn Development Corporation, who published a report in *Current Archaeology* in March, 1972. The broken and unbroken tiles (and a number of sandstone coffins) were then 'lifted' for conservation by the Ancient Monuments Section of the Department of the Environment and for eventual display 'under suitable museum conditions'. During the first excavation 'the possible site of the kiln in which the tiles were fired' was noted.

Tiles of several kinds were found, the largest group being an interrupted area of mosaic, totalling 'seventy square metres' (approximately eighty-four square yards), concentrated at the east end of the nave and in the adjacent north and south transepts of the lost church. They were laid there after its extension in the early fourteenth century. In addition, lying loose were some 'square line-impressed tiles with designs which included lion faces, foliage and geometric shapes', clearly reminiscent of square tiles at Icklingham All Saints (see below). Some later figured slip tiles were found and 'several square metres of a 15th century tile floor', composed of 'relief decorated tiles, yellow and black, with linking geometric decoration'. The mosaic tiles were made in *sixteen* different shapes, some with extra line-impressed ornament, and were coloured yellow (over slip), black or green. They had first suffered two hundred years' wear, then damage when the church was demolished after the Dissolution and, finally, disturbance by 'gardening activities'. Thus, much colour had disappeared and many tiles lay *in situ* but cracked into fragments. There remained, though, sufficient detail to suggest the 'dazzling display' lost.

Perhaps the least remarkable thing about these exciting tile discoveries is the number of decorative methods and periods: from Rievaulx to St. Albans, the premier abbey, or even Little Coggeshall in Essex, the monasteries appear as users of successive methods of tile decoration, for different floors at the same place. The most remarkable features are the use of a genuine black, both for the mosaic and the later relief tiles; the appearance of unique mosaic shapes, such as the chains of 'lemons', 'with and without quatrefoil centres'; the appearance, so far beyond East Anglia, of line-impressed motifs – mostly rosettes and the remarkable (unique) thick 'Y's' round the six-petalled black flowers, besides the larger motifs on the square tiles. In addition, the use of relief work as late as the fifteenth century is unexpected, seeming still more conservative because of its 'linking geometric decoration'.

The mosaic shares elements with the Ely or eastern group. It has some similar shapes, such as the stars and the large flowers, which are formed in different ways. Despite the large number of unusual shapes, though, the Runcorn pavement was less elaborate than either the Crauden mosaic or classic Cistercian. It was laid in panels, the variety simple rather than complex, for they included 'square tiles laid in diagonal rows', 'square and rectangular tiles in a "woven" pattern' and 'octagonal tiles with quatrefoil centres'. Even the unusual shapes, such as the 'elongated quatrefoil flowers', 'small quatrefoil flowers of two types' and trefoils, are less elaborate than Ely's central chain, while Meaux Abbey could produce fifty different shapes at that period. There are no figures, in contrast to Ely and Meesden.

Arguably, the most sophisticated item is the black colouring. This is remarkably distinct from the green and was partly, and surprisingly, achieved by using both an unusual glaze and a darker clay. It seems best to quote, gratefully, from a letter from Mr. Greene (9 May 1973): 'The composition of the black glaze ... is uncertain and research is at present being done ... by an analytical team from a local chemical firm. I expect that the results of the research will show that it is a lead glaze containing high levels of copper ... there is a distinct difference in the clay used for dark tiles and light glazed tiles ... the mediaeval tile makers seem, therefore, to have used clay that would enhance the colour of the glaze.' The Crauden mosaic and its closer relations consist mainly of yellow-glazed slip tiles and glazed earthenware (brown). Some green slip tiles were used, but no black.

Mosaic with line-impressed motifs was laid at Little Coggeshall Abbey in Essex, a Cistercian house from 1148. Notable and pioneering brickwork remains there, but the tiles are known mainly from a nineteenth-century record and from scattered excavation finds. The facts are given in the article by J. S. Gardner, 'Coggeshall Abbey and Its Early Brickwork', in the *Journal of the British Archaeological Association* 1955.

The excavators discovered some of the fourteenth-century mosaic tiles and also figured slip tiles, the designs of these including geometric patterns and heraldry – unusual but not very sophisticated. In addition, there survives inside the south door of the extant St. Nicholas' Chapel (the *capella extra portas*, once outside the abbey's gates) a small worn strip of mosaic: this is composed of two forms only, 'rectangles' with two concave corners and circles to fit into them. In 1860, though, 'an elaborate pavement' was uncovered in the chapel, only to be destroyed. A coloured drawing was made, recording its layout and revealing the close likeness to Ely's Crauden pavement. The excavation of the abbey site showed that similar mosaic was laid in other buildings, but Ely-style irregular mosaic was not found. The Victorian destruction seems especially unforgivable, since the mosaic was evidently well-preserved. The drawing recorded a circular pattern very like the side panels of the nave in Crauden's chapel. The main difference was the greater use at Coggeshall of line-impressed details, including tiny motifs not (or perhaps no longer) seen at Ely – trefoils, quatrefoils, triple rosettes. Even the borders to the circles were marked with these, and the larger ones were used in place of small separate tiles at Ely. What the practical connection was between the two sets of mosaic – at a small Cistercian house and a large Benedictine one – is unknown, but Ely may be presumed the inspirer. The tiles were certainly fired near their own sites.

At Icklingham All Saints' Church in Suffolk it is clear that the Benedictine abbey at Ely acted as the supplier. There are at Icklingham, though, large and small square tiles with line-impressed motifs not featured at Ely. These are the clumsy faces, birds in circles, the trefoils and other compass-drawn designs and the flamboyant crocketed pinnacles or canopies, a group of designs reminiscent of the new finds at Runcorn.

Icklingham, described by Norman Scarfe in the *Shell Guide* to Suffolk as a 'beautiful unrestored church', is now locked up and classed as redundant. It is situated in the Breckland, on a tributary of Ely's Ouse. Much of the building was done in the early fourteenth century, the tiles being contemporary with the chancel where they are set – though Scarfe notes their arrangement is 'somewhat Victorian'. As at Ely, the glaze and thus most of the colour has worn away. The impressed motifs listed above and the square and rectangular tiles they ornament represent work not surviving anywhere at Ely itself. What is exactly duplicated is the polychrome mosaic of the Crauden side panels, with the simpler circular pattern, which is composed of five different shapes with line-impressed rosettes on some.

ICKLINGHAM ALL SAINTS CHURCH, SUFFOLK Fourteenth-century mosaic of circular pattern, with line-impressed details, similar to mosaic of Prior Crauden's Chapel at Ely.

In Ely Cathedral itself, centre of the great monastery and of the diocese, there must once have been many decorated floors – probably both of mosaic and of later figured tiles. The only survivor is an area of about sixteen by nine feet in the south transept, hidden now under a mat and seats. The tiles are seemingly of the fourteenth century and of geometrical design only, but have lost all colouring. Most are seven inches square, bearing a simple four-lobed shape – also used inside the curved octagonal tiles of the main Crauden mosaic. In the centre is a circle formed of segmental tiles.

This paving may have been part of a more elaborate floor: John Gough Nichols, whose *Examples of Decorative Tiles* was published in 1845, said the south transept had mosaic of the same type as Prior Crauden's and compared both with a pavement found at Louth in Lincolnshire. The Louth floor, which had been found during repairs to the house of a local M.P., was described in the *Gentleman's Magazine* in 1801 (page 1161). That report gave little detail, but there was an engraved illustration. The pavement was circular, sixteen-

89

and-a-half feet in diameter, but probably incomplete. In the middle was a circular design made of rectangular and segmental tiles, quite like the south transept's. The wide outer border was made of small skewed diamonds, a shape used for line-impressed border tiles in the Crauden chapel. Between these two groups was the main design, a circular arcade of columns carrying intersecting arches. The style of the arcade is plain Early English (of the thirteenth century), though the pavement was most likely later. The engraver did not indicate how the arcade tiles were shaped.

Nichols said that there were also remains in the south transept at Ely of irregular mosaic figures, like Crauden's. All in all, it seems unlikely that Crauden's complex mosaic was confined to one small chapel, however special, in the Ely Close – especially since Icklingham and Coggeshall share some of its elements.

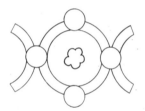

(*c*) PRIOR CRAUDEN'S PAVEMENT AT ELY

The early fourteenth-century pavement at Ely is unique in its completeness and variety, though it has lost most of its colouring. Many stamped linear motifs and the *sgraffito* details, incised freehand with some sort of metal stylus, have also been worn away. While it is not unique in all its parts, close relations are few and the irregular mosaic panels have no rivals. These figured panels are set out like heavy mediaeval painted glass, with *sgraffito* details in slip – most like, but the reverse of, the 'white' scraped details in later mediaeval glass – and with mortar joints instead of lead divisions. It is a particular shame that nearly all colour and differentiation has gone from the figures. The poke-nosed dragon, for example, is now rendered almost invisible: one finds it first in the early nineteenth-century coloured

90

print and only then in the floor itself. The print reveals other losses, especially of line-impressed rosettes and cinquefoils, and the reduction of the green colouring – now limited mainly to the edges of the floor. Among the inlaid tiles of the outer border it is now difficult to find good examples of the spreadeagle design. The mosaic still appears dark and light (helped by waxing), but the brown is muted to chestnut or earthenware and the yellow survives only in traces, though parts of the floor by the west and side walls retain brighter colouring.

This is, says Professor Pevsner, 'one of the most important tile mosaic pavements of England'. It is still absorbing, but of all the mediaeval tile floors, this is the one one would most like to see new. It is unbearable not to be able to move out the small benches and see the long-lost colours return.

The setting is also battered but spectacular, with contemporary carved stone decoration and some old glass surviving. The treasurer of the Benedictine abbey recorded expenditure on the building of the chapel in 1324–25 for Prior John de Crauden ('Johannes de Crawedene'). It was erected over a low, dark thirteenth-century undercroft, so that one makes a narrow ascent into the light of the big windows above. The chapel is about twice as high as the lower chamber, proportions like those of the great Sainte Chapelle in Paris. The decorated tracery of the windows and the rich flamboyant carving of the niches in the side walls and flanking the altar harmonise with the truly complex pavement. The tiles cover the whole floor of twenty feet nine inches by thirteen feet seven inches, though there have been slight losses at the north side. There are even mosaic stars and hexagons on the riser of the step to the altar platform, which is slightly narrower than the nave.

Despite the correspondence in style and vigour between the stone carving and the patterned tiles, the stonework is the place mainly of faces, flowers and leaves and the pavement is the place mainly of geometry and of fauna. The pavement combines five techniques: regular abstract and interlocking mosaic with line-impressed extras, irregular mosaic with drawn details and – the technique of the future – slip inlays. The larger heraldic lions as well as the figures and trees of the 'Temptation' panel have *sgraffito* work. The inlaid tiles, five inches square and bearing lions, stags and eagles, are limited to the north and south borders and are, thus, mostly in good condition. The climax of the pavement is the tile picture in the centre of the altar

91

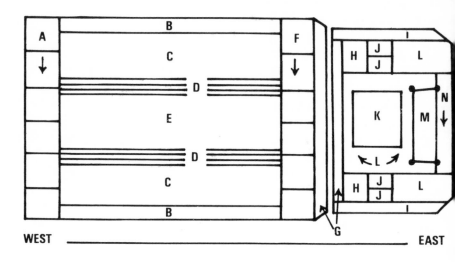

29   PLAN OF PAVEMENT IN PRIOR CRAUDEN'S CHAPEL

A Row of six 'passant gardant' lions (with one paw raised) in irregular mosaic. (They are to be looked at facing west, the only figured tiles in the pavement set this way.)

B Border strip of lozenge-shaped and small inlaid tiles, with animal motifs (eagle, lion, stag).

C Panels of mosaic with circular pattern.

D Mosaic strip, including six-pointed stars.

E Central panel of mosaic, based on interlocking circles.

F Row of large, irregular mosaic lions (as A) with one panel of dragon.

G Small mosaic tiles.

H Large lions (as A and F).

I Small inlaid tiles (as B).

J Smaller lions, in irregular mosaic.

K 'Temptation' panel, about 44 by 32 inches, of irregular mosaic with *sgraffito* details.

L Mosaic, including stars (as D).

M (Altar)

N Mosaic, including circles.

Note The whole floor, including the altar platform, measures about 20 ft 9 ins by 13 ft 7 ins.

92

platform, a worn panel of about forty-four by thirty-two inches, showing the Temptation of Adam and Eve by the Serpent. The platform constitutes about a quarter of the floor and some of its tiles are better preserved, retaining much of the glaze so that the effect is sharper. Brown (self-colour) is the dominant colour throughout the floor, usually opposed to yellow slip-coated tiles. In the geometrical mosaic light and dark do not rigidly alternate, because of the number of different shapes used in each panel. There is no other floor of this complexity, even at the technical level of mixing techniques. It is a virtuoso layout, grand rather than pretty – though the Eve has the wistful naïveté of some teenage idol.

The surviving records are minimal, though much is known of the costs of the other abbey buildings and of the cathedral. When F. R. Chapman published the *Sacrist Rolls of Ely Cathedral* in two volumes in 1907, he could mention only a brief note concerning this chapel, made on an inventory by the abbey's treasurer in 1324–25. This read, *In noua constructione capelle et camere Domini Prioris* ... 138*li.* 8*s.* 5*d.*: 'towards the building of the new chapel and study (literally, room) ... £138 8s. 5d.' In modern money, this perhaps represents £7,000. Part of the study, including a fireplace, remains, attached to the 'prior's house'. Crauden was Prior from 1321, his period of office starting in the same year as that of Alan of Walsingham, the sacrist and mason. Crauden was the effective leader of the abbey at the peak of its activities, symbolised by the great timber lantern over the cathedral crossing. The Lady Chapel's foundation stone was laid in 1321. Crauden died in 1341, and was buried in the cathedral. In the *Liber Eliensis*, a fifteenth-century history of Ely's bishops, or secular abbots, Crauden's new chapel was described as being 'of wondrous beauty' (*mirandi decoris*). He prayed by day and by night there ('he was accustomed to rise by night and seek the Chapel alone'), 'unless hindered by grievous sickness', and its altar light was visible from his study. Thus we have recorded the love that went into the building and its embellishment, but we lack practical information or even a note of the cost of the tiles – which we can assume were designed and made at Ely.

The main floor has three strips of mosaic, with two different circular designs in which circles and curved diamonds and octagons are dominant. The narrow dividing strips (west to east) are composed of six-pointed stars. At east and west are rows of large heraldic lions, of

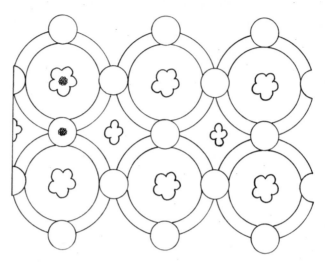

Side panel: the diameter of the large circles is $8\frac{1}{2}$ inches. (Mosaic duplicated at Icklingham All Saints, Suffolk.)

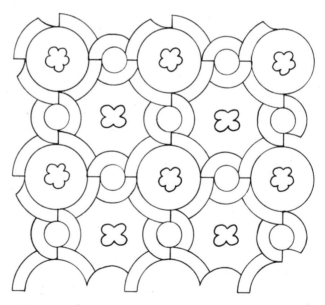

Central panel, with 'chains' of interlocking circles. The diameter of the large circles is $7\frac{1}{2}$ inches.

irregular mosaic, while the south and north borders have a complicated mixture of triangles, skewed lozenges (rhomboids) and the inlaid tiles. The same shapes appear on the altar platform, where the three-fold division is maintained, the Temptation taking up the front half of the wide central slip. Round this panel there is mosaic with stars, and to the side are large and small mosaic lions.

Two circular patterns constitute the bulk of the mosaic. The largest tiles are dark. Their circular borders and flower centres were slip-coated and have, or had, stamped rosettes. The more complex and delicate pattern, with links like chains, is limited to the central panel of the nave. It has seven mosaic shapes, including cusped hollow circles seven-and-a-half inches in diameter; the cinquefoils that fit into these; concave octagons; small circles two-and-three-quarter inches across; circular border segments, one-and-a-half inches wide. The twin side panels have five different shapes, used also at the east end (and see also Icklingham, Suffolk). Measurements are rather thicker: the hollow circles are eight-and-a-half inches in diameter; the plain circles three-and-three-quarter inches in diameter; the circular border strips two inches across. From loose tiles one sees that thicknesses vary: the hollow curved lozenges (side panels) are one-and-a-third inches thick and their quatrefoil centres just an inch thick. Perfect firing of the interlocking pieces must have been difficult to achieve, and with the irregular mosaic results had to be even enough, for example, for the components of the smaller lions to be layable either way up – so that these beasts could confront each other with paws raised as if to strike.

There were likenesses between the circular or chain mosaic of Rievaulx (say) and of Ely, but this floor goes beyond the Cistercian work: it does not excel in the number of different shapes but in the number of techniques, and especially in the free style of the irregular slip-coated mosaic. These 'pictorial' panels take up a fairly small proportion of the floor, but their effect is still dramatic and they must surely be the representatives of a lost class. The pieces for the scene of the Fall of Man would have been cut freehand, but those for the lions must have been cut round a template (or moulded). Their very irregularity of line and the reliance on *sgraffito* for the finer markings made them most prone to wear – and this to the point that they may now demand some imaginative effort, a visualised restoration.

Only yellow is used for the lions. Made in one piece, the larger

31 'TEMPTATION' PANEL
Tile picture of Adam and Eve with the serpent, Prior Crauden's Chapel, Ely, about 1325. (44 inches by 32 inches.)

lions stretch out in heraldic pose, *passant guardant*, looking outwards with one paw raised. Incised lines mark their manes, plumy curled tails, hairy legs and paws. Standing upright, the smaller lions are confined to the altar platform and are very worn. They are formed of irregular or broken mosaic in panels about one-and-a-half feet square, again with *sgraffito* hair. Centrally below the altar step is the one dragon panel, measuring one foot four inches by one foot one-and-a-half inches. The creature is reduced to earthenware and outline. It is made of seven wholly uneven pieces, with bat wings and a strange bulge for the coiled tail. It is chunky and literally backward-looking, an endearing relative of the dragons reduced in mediaeval paintings to docile, improbable pets for virgins rescued by St. George. The creature may have been a cross-reference to the Temptation, with the Devil as serpent or dragon.

96

The Temptation scene is indeniably interesting and even moving, although it now appears fairly crude or heavy in execution. Not far off four by three feet, it is made of quite large pieces. Wear has been great, as can be seen from the nineteenth-century print and even from a not very old photograph, so the panel should be protected. Originally only the background was plain. The pieces for the figures were thickly slip-coated and glazed yellow, while the trunk and formalised foliage of the tree were lightly coated and glazed a suitably pale or leaf green. Both the figures and the tree with its bunches of leaves and round fruits, are deeply lined and outlined because of the mosaic pieces. The extra details drawn in the slip were mainly for the leaves and parts of figures – toes, fingers, faces, hair. The Serpent has the face and bust of a woman, apparently assumed at the most critical or crucial times. It wreathes round the tree to face Eve. Adam holds a fruit to his lips, while Eve holds out a second fruit to him. Physically the figures are scarcely distinguished, but Eve is slimmer and has trailing hair. She is a 'slip of a girl', with wide eyes and seeming resignation in her expression. Remove this authenticity of feeling, and we have only a vigorous and fascinating display of craftsmanship. The main mosaic, with its fairly intricate but neat interlocking circles, is more skilled work. In this whole wonderful pavement, though, Eve's vulnerability stimulates the sole emotionally immediate response.

(*d*) BORDESLEY AND MEESDEN

The oldest Cistercian mosaic had included as minor items rosettes formed of slip inlay. The earliest inlaid and secular floors, excavated at the thirteenth-century palace of Clarendon in Wiltshire, retained a mosaic element in that rectangular and segmental tiles were used as well as the squares that would become *the* shape for decorated tiles. The roughly contemporary Chertsey Abbey tiles included little

97

rectangles bearing individual inlaid letters, for inscriptions, and the famous roundels with their polygonal surrounds. Their inlaid designs, however, dominate the Clarendon and Chertsey tiles: they may be, strictly, inlaid mosaic but one tends to think of them just as inlaid. Some of the soon-abandoned possibilities of mixing techniques can be shown rather better by two dissimilar pavements of lesser importance, both of the fourteenth century.

The Bordesley pavement is a nineteenth-century reconstruction, consisting of worn tiles taken from the site of Bordesley Abbey at Tardebrigge and laid in the vestry of St. Stephen's Church (1855) at Church Green in Redditch, Worcestershire. They are now protected by a carpet. Since pavements from this Cistercian abbey were being sold off at 5s. each as early as 1538, the survivals are remarkable. New excavation of the site, begun in 1968, has revealed clear traces of removed tiles and also further tiles, in better condition and including figures – such as a seated man with a dog. There is a report that a set of sixteen heraldic tiles were found during the nineteenth-century excavations, but these did not reach the new church. Tiles as well as building stones from the abbey were said to be in local houses.

What the relaid pavement shows is a type of work, inlaid or semi-mosaic, intervening between true mosaic – the traditional Cistercian style – and the unvaried use of square figured tiles (perhaps with plain borders). The St. Stephen's tiles may not, of course, all have come from the same original pavement and the Victorians might have abandoned single-colour mosaic or squares as too worn or uninteresting. There are finely-inlaid border tiles, measuring five-and-a-half by three inches, with a stylised foliage pattern. There are hexagonal tiles, their sides measuring six, three-and-a-half and two inches, each bearing a fleur-de-lis, a bar and a four-petalled flower. There are tiles of three-and-a-half and five-and-a-half inches square, mostly the larger size and mostly quadrants with foliage and fleurs-de-lis and a fine-lined geometric or abstract pattern, which is surprisingly classical. Fitted round the hexagonal tiles are squares with an odd fussy design: they have a tiny square in the centre and in the corners a splayed cross ('cross paty' or 'formy', except that it has rounded instead of straight ends), a flower, a double-circle and a twelve-pointed star. These tiny studlike motifs remind one of the larger line-impressed rosettes at Meesden and in Prior Crauden's pavement at Ely.

Whenever tiles need their neighbours to complete a design we

32   Fourteenth-century inlaid tiles, with mosaic elements, from Bordesley Abbey,
now in St. Stephen's Church at Redditch, Worcestershire. (*Not to scale*).
(a) Border tiles.
(b) $5\frac{1}{2}$ inch square tiles with repeating patterns.
(c) Mosaic tiles with inlaid designs.

perhaps have the surviving influence of mosaic. This applies here to the quadrant patterns, which have to be set in groups of at least four, and to the run-on foliage design of the borders, similar to early Wessex borders and also to some relief designs. The inlays at Redditch look backwards to the fine Wessex tiles and forward to the Penn types, with their thicker inlays and repeating patterns. A foliate fleur-de-lis in a circle is reminiscent of Wessex, but most of the foliage is like Penn's. Thus this battered grouping, probably of mid-fourteenth-century tiles, is transitional in style as well as technique.

The sanctuary pavement at Meesden is of near-abstract mosaic, shining and coherent, a rare survival in a very isolated Hertfordshire church. The chancel dates from about 1300, while the pavement looks early or mid-fourteenth-century. It is in a sense conservative, for mosaic is still dominant, though supplemented throughout by line-impressed details – such as a cross paty like Bordesley's – and also by some square inlaid tiles in the outer border. The village location alone implies that so rich a pavement, unusual even in its colours of yellow and deep green, cannot have been unique. Its presence may be explained by local connections with the important but late Cistercian abbey of St. Mary Graces in the City of London. Would not London, at least, have had work of this kind, a development going beyond the Yorkshire-type mosaic? If St. Mary Graces was involved at Meesden, though, the pavement must date from after 1350 – the abbey's foundation.

In the thirteenth and fourteenth centuries the patrons of the church belonged to the Monchesey family, and the inlaid work includes their arms (alone), done in the simplified colouring of tiles. Technically these arms were 'barry vair and gules', that is red bars dividing bands of 'vair'. Vair is an undulating pattern of dark (blue) and light (white, for silver), familiar from the grey or blue and white fur linings of the cloaks of the great – which are seen in mediaeval paintings and manuscripts.

Stylistically the Meesden pavement has links with Ely's, though the pieces are smaller and more delicate. Meesden has line-impressed rosettes, though with more petals. There are pairs of facing birds, as at Icklingham All Saints in Suffolk (supplied by Ely), but a better design and inlaid. Meesden and Ely both have small inlaid lions. The mixture of techniques itself is common, and some of the shapes in the wide surround to the Meesden wheel are similar to Ely's, including the

100

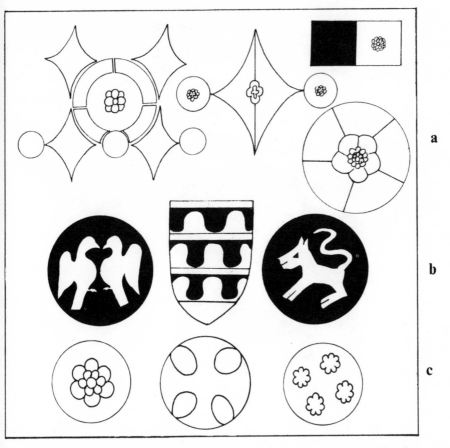

a

b

c

33   Fourteenth-century pavement of yellow and green mosaic tiles at Meesden
Church, Hertfordshire. (*Not to scale.*)
(a) Mosaic tiles from border.
(b) Inlaid details.
(c) Line-impressed details.

'flowers' with edges like thick serrated pastry. No likeness, however,
encroaches on the glazed colours – but Ely's are disadvantaged by
heavy wear – or on the splendid central wheel at Meesden. (If you
are inspired to go to Meesden, do avoid treading on the tiles, and make
some contribution to the fabric fund.)

The complete pavement measures about nine by seven feet. Yellow
and rich green alternate, elegantly precise. The spokes of the wheel
spread out like wide neckties. Each spoke is made of six different

101

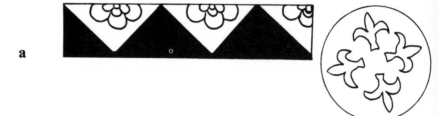

a

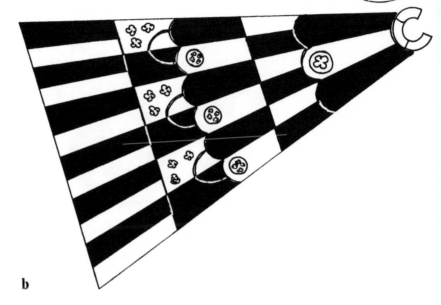

b

34   Mosaic shapes forming main design of a wheel in Meesden Church pavement, Hertfordshire. (*Not to scale.*)
(a) Triangular tiles from border, with round tile at centre of wheel.
(b) Six mosaic shapes used for 'spokes' of wheel.

mosaic shapes, two of them rounded like key tags. At the centre is one round tile with four fleurs-de-lis, line-impressed. Most of the yellow tiles, but none of the green, have line-impressed rosettes. Triangular tiles border the wheel and then there is a wide band of mosaic, mostly curved diamonds, roundels and segments of roundels. The outer border has the inlaid designs, the only figures: Monchesey arms; pairs of birds; a lion with a flyaway tail. The complexity of the mosaic composition is revelatory. The effect achieved was lovely, and is now much more than rare.

102

CHAPTER FIVE

The two-colour majority: the main schools and their designs

(*a*) CHERTSEY AND WESTMINSTER

From their rediscovery in the last century this has been the most praised school of tiles, seen as constituting 'the high-watermark of of mediaeval tile manufacture' (J. B. Ward-Perkins). The Surrey abbey's tiles themselves were rediscovered through several excavations, though the finds from the first one – in 1853 – were immediately stolen. Rather earlier, the planks had been taken off the Westminster Abbey Chapter House pavement – and Minton replicas were on sale from 1841 or 1842. With the big exception of the Westminster pavement, this is also the most fragmented and frustrating group of tiles. Examples, whole and broken, are scattered between museums and perhaps also in inaccessible private houses. The church of Little Kimble in Buckinghamshire has had six pictorial Chertsey tiles since 1872. Some Chertsey tiles were last heard of gracing a Victorian summer-house. Apart from the samples removed then, the related tiles of Halesowen Abbey in Warwickshire lie under two feet of soil and were last seen a hundred years ago.

These tiles belonged to the later thirteenth-century surge of artistic activity that was centred on Henry III's rebuilding and decoration of Westminster Abbey and on his Westminster and country palaces. There was a court style of painting, of which examples remain in the Abbey, with swaying, almost mannerist, figures of saints – like the St. Peter with pointing fingers and a great key,

103

painted on an altar panel in the south ambulatory. Beautiful figures carved in soft stone have also survived, but with draperies worn or broken. Wall paintings with mythological and romance subjects have vanished with the palaces, but have left traces of these subjects in the royal account rolls. Fine ironwork was made, which covered the thick wooden doors with vine scrolls, like that of the Henry III door by Gilbertus in St. George's Chapel at Windsor Castle. (This would be followed later in the century by the sophisticated work of Thomas of Leighton [Leighton Buzzard], maker of the Eleanor grille at Westminster.) The Clarendon Palace and other Wessex tiles, despite their dragons and griffins, are by comparison simple, but the finer-lined and more intense Chertsey tiles may be attached to the court style. It is fascinating to see in these the pointed turret roofs, strong masonry lines, narrow round-headed windows and scroll-ornamented doors – and even the big door key held in the hand of an anxious character in the Tristam and Isolde story – that we find in contemporary paintings and drawings of the great abbey and other buildings.

Even the tiles' griffins, dragons and curvetting centaurs have a sort of contemporary match in animal strangeness, seen in the famous picture in the chronicles of Matthew Paris, in the elephant given by Louis IX of France to Henry III. The Emperor Frederick II, too, in 1235, had sent Henry three leopards in token of the English royal arms, in the earlier version – as seen on tiles at Cleeve Abbey, Somerset. These leopards were kept at the Tower of London. The three lions of the Westminster tiles are, in fact, very early examples of this later standard version. A royal menagerie was kept at the Tower from the thirteenth or fourteenth century until 1834.

A miniature Renaissance is suggested by such designs as the acanthus and leaf-based palmette border tiles of the Westminster pavement, the acanthus capitals of columns and segmental acanthus borders in Chertsey's own pictorial tiles, as well as the use of a variant of the angular classical 'key' pattern. There is an example of this last in the site museum at Hailes Abbey in Gloucestershire, which has a few Chertsey tiles. The closest associations are with contemporary manuscripts, both English and French. So much so that the criteria assumed for the most complex or detailed Chertsey tiles are perhaps those of manuscript illumination and not – for all their beauty and technical accomplishment – specifically those of tile design. To take these early and court-style inlaid tiles as a peak to be followed by a long low trough is to give English figured tile-making altogether too brief a summer; more commonly as well as appropriately the good decorated floor tiles, that can still be appreciated without detective work, achieve the artistic standards and aesthetic pleasures of a craft and not of painting. The small grotesque creatures among the veined oak leaves and foliage scrolls, the dragons with women's faces and headdresses who frame the pictorial roundels, have close relations in contemporary manuscripts – the sharp-eyed grotesqueries in the margins, who inhabit the acanthus leaves of French manuscripts and the more usual vine scrolls of English manuscripts. Margaret Rickert (in *Painting in Britain: The Middle Ages*, 1954) compares the Chertsey designs with the work of Matthew Paris and the St. Albans Abbey limners. The design of Richard I charging to combat she compares more precisely with fight scenes in *La Estoire de Seint Aedward le Rei* (manuscript in Cambridge University Library) and their versions of St. John's vision of the Apocalypse.

The main group of these tiles were made at the Benedictine abbey of Chertsey in the 1260s or 1270s. The abbey enjoyed royal patronage, as did Hailes. No tiles remain at its site, but the new museum in Windsor Street has examples and so do the museums at Guildford and Weybridge. There were said to be some at Alm'ners Priory, Lyne, and 'several other places' locally, but Alm'ners anyway – which used to have a showcase with tiles – has none now. The Victoria & Albert Museum has a few, but the great bulk of the discoveries, published by Shurlock in 1885 (see the Booklist), belong to the British Museum.

Although these were inlaid tiles, a fair number of different shapes were used, including small wedge or segmental tiles made to carry one, two or three Lombardic letters. These were for inscriptions to outline the pictorial roundels, Latin REX, LEO and RICA for the tiles of Richard the Lionheart, who had died in 1199, and Norman–French labels for the long Tristram series, which shows the Arthurian romance of the knight Tristram, Isolde (YSOUDE) and the deceived King Mark (MARC) of Cornwall. The roundels are nine to ten inches across, being set between four heptagonal tiles that make up a sixteen-inch square. Which borders went with which pictorial roundels has been the product of Victorian and later guesswork, but the favourite motifs for the borders were a ring of women-faced dragons with densely spreading oak leaves in the spandrels. Among the polygonal tiles are

105

35   CHERTSEY TILES OF
ABOUT 1255 IN WEST-
MINSTER ABBEY CHAPTER
HOUSE
Tile design of Edward the
Confessor and the pil-
grim (7 inches square).

Four-tile set, with royal
arms, dragons and cen-
taurs (each 10 inches
square).

Border tile, pike (8 by
$3\frac{1}{2}$ inches).

'cowhide' or cusped octagonal shapes round which small circles were fitted, and big hexagons like primitive axe heads – these inlaid with beautiful foliage scrolls with grapes or berries, four of these converging on a tiny roundel of a lion or on a rosette.

Thirty-four pictures have been identified as belonging to the Tristram series and there are extra 'unidentifiable' fragments. The six tiles at Little Kimble belong to this series. Besides the story's characters – among whom the laymen, such as court musicians, wear round tasselled caps – we see ships, buildings and contemporary furniture and fittings, such as Mark's throne and cushion. The clarity and detail is exceptional. Mrs Eames describes the scenes as being 'drawn by a first class artist' but probably to illustrate a lost manuscript, rather than designed specially for the tiles. Among the Chertsey roundels are two separate ones for the single combat in which the king killed Saladin, who is pierced through with the lance, and up to seven further scenes which may show incidents in Richard's history. They are all rich in movement, combative or hunting scenes – such as a man fighting a lion.

These elaborately framed roundels were the highlights – like *oeillets* or peepholes opening on the legendary action – in honey-and-russet coloured pavements of inlaid mosaic in the main less free and less complex. Henry III ordered murals of the *duellum Regis Ricardi* for his own chamber at Clarendon in Wiltshire and it is inconceivable that he and the court audience lacked a set of the Lionheart tiles and the Tristram series, laid within a few years of Henry's marriage to Eleanor of Provence in 1254. It is most likely that they were set in pavements at the palace of Westminster itself, which was abandoned in 1529 by Henry VIII for Wolsey's York House – or Whitehall – to the north.

The virtually intact pavement in the Chapter, or meeting house, of Westminster Abbey has the artistic merit of greater simplicity. It has also only a small 'religious' element – and some of that is open to 'demotion' for various reasons, if we attempt the precise, probably inappropriate, distinction between spiritual and secular *content* regardless of intention. (This part of the abbey is looked after by the State, through the Department of the Environment: there is a guide-book, by J. G. Noppen, revised by S. E. Rigold. In the antechamber are Victorian replicas of later mediaeval tiles.)

The inlaid figuration has largely kept its original tawny colour in a ground like brown amber, though some tiles – especially those with thin leafy fleurs-de-lis – are worn. No plain tiles were used. Although the designs are fine and narrow-lined the inlay is deep. Only a tiny number of the tiles are modern replacements. The pavement is very big – fifty feet across from the north to the south wall – and octagonal to fit the shape of the building. The chronicler Matthew Paris said 'the king has built an incomparable chapter house'. The building had been started in about 1245, while the pavement could have been laid down ten or a dozen years later. In 1258 it was directed that the residue of the Chapter House tiles be laid elsewhere. Along the south-east edge was set a dedication, made with small rectangular tiles with plump Lombardic letters. The opening lines, *Ut rosa flos florum/sic est domus ista domorum*, are known also from the octagonal Chapter House of York Minster. The inscription, as far as it could be read, has been translated *As the rose is the flower of flowers,/so this house is the house of houses,/which King Henry, the friend of the Holy Trinity, dedicated to Christ who loved* ... The damage to the stone carving, the necessary but steely total restoration of the rib-vaulted roof by Gilbert Scott in 1866 and the deterioration (and different dates) of the paintings on the walls have left the floor as now the most consistent and vivid part of the 'incomparable' council chamber of these royally-provided Benedictines.

The pavement is set out in grand long panels, east to west. There are twelve of them, composed of tiles between six and ten inches square. The bulk of these, whether distinct designs or incomplete quadrants, are laid in radiating sets of four. Between the panels run rows of narrow rectangular division tiles, of different sizes up to eight by four inches. In the main the layout is regular, with one pattern to a panel, though the beautiful largest quadrants, which form the royal arms, take up two separate panels and one panel is shared by lions (at the west end) and griffins. The octagonal ground-plan and the presence of the central column meant that there were needed – at the edges of the floor and round the base of the column – some small makeweight tiles, wedge-shaped or trapezi-form: for these the smaller Greek-style pattern, based on honeysuckle, was normally employed (at the wide end), along with a varying number of roughly-cut suns or stars.

The main breaks or intrusions in the layout are the bands of pic-torial tiles, running north to south in the southern half of the pavement, and two blocks of rose windows, which are set along the eastern edge and in the north-east corner. The roses are lovely: their circles of pointed lights, framed by quatrefoils and triangles, are formed by quadrant tiles seven inches square. It is thought they were inspired by the contemporary windows of the abbey's south transept – lost windows twice replaced in modern times. They are, in fact, much like a cut-down, simpler version of the great thirteenth-century rose window in the south transept of Notre-Dame, Paris. These tiles are forerunners of the window tracery patterns in Sebrok's pavement, Gloucester Cathedral, and of the smaller elaborate roses at Great Malvern, both fifteenth-century. There are eight of the intrusive pictorial designs, seven inches square, with a few repeats. They are very close in style to the slightly later Tristram and Richard roundels from Chertsey. Besides a stag-hunting scene with horseman, bowman and dogs, running over three tiles, these are the figures: Edward the Confessor and the pilgrim; the King, enthroned with a pet dog; the Queen, similarly enthroned, with a hawk on her wrist; a mitred ecclesiastic; two musicians, playing harp and rebeck (an early violin), very like a Tristram scene. It is convincingly argued now that these tiles are later insertions, being surplus stock, really designed for a palace floor. (There has also been some disturbance of the tiles below them, in the south-west corner of the pavement.) Most of them are particularly badly worn.

Apart from these exceptional small groups, this is a pavement wholly figured with animals and foliage, whose designs are scattered over a scale between naturalism and formalism. There are some twenty designs in all. The mythological animals include pairs of high-winged griffins and, a single group only, more sinister basilisks with a second face attached to their tails. Frivolously, dragons and centaurs (half-man, half-horse) border the heraldic shield of Henry III, with its three graduated fierce and curly-maned lions, the whole four-tile group being some twenty inches square. Pairs of subtle-limbed leopards or lionesses, addorsed (or back-to-back) wreathe their tails together: four tiles make a circle of eight of them. Cuddly, open-mouthed small lions in single pairs, also addorsed, share a large sycamore leaf as a plume to their tails. On quadrant tiles the fox creeps up on the careless fine-feathered cock (four of each in a quatrefoil), a favourite scene in manuscript illumination also: more 'real' than the invented and foreign animals, this tile design is yet stylised in its details.

(a) Border tile, 6 by 2 inches.

(c) Border tile, 6 by 3 inches.

(b) Border tile, 8 by 4 inches.

37   Fourteenth-century printed tile, $4\frac{1}{2}$ inches square, in St. Faith's Chapel at Westminster Abbey. The objects are probably pricket-type candlesticks.

The twin voracious-jawed, scaly pikes are striking designs, perhaps the most realistic – if not quite naturalistic – of the fauna and indeed of all the designs. (The literary nonsense about these being St. Peter's salmon should be discounted.) They are on border tiles of eight by four inches, used frequently and in confrontation. Interestingly, we can see tiny accidental differences between the cut of the design stamps: the left fish has longer jaws, more lines at the gills and scales reaching closer to the line of the back.

. A dozen different foliage patterns are used, both on six- or eight-inch squares, and supplying the great majority of the division tiles. Again there are varying degrees of naturalism. There are three big patterns of fleurs-de-lis set in circles, the most foliate one being like a thirteenth-century relief design at Abbey Dore in Herefordshire. There are smaller tiles with more or less stylised leaf designs, one with little trefoils and fleurs-de-lis, like a thinner version of a later Penn design, and another of fairly realistic oak leaves set in a circle.

Highly stylised and remarkably Greek is the six by two inch border tile design of the palmette, distantly based on palm branches. It is used singly or occasionally doubly, for a square tile, as well as for the irregular makeweights. The other Greek design, slightly larger (six by three inches) is the curling acanthus-like pattern of honeysuckle (anthemion), reduced versions of which supply the capitals of columns in the pictorial tiles, besides capitals, royal crowns and roundel borders to the later Chertsey tiles – the most nearly exact correspondence between the two groups.

Formed in quite a different way is the close- and fine-lined foliage scroll, used on border tiles of eight by four inches. This sophisticated pattern is like some of the small-leaved scrollwork in later mediaeval French illuminated manuscripts. Against five other patterns it was chosen for seven of the long borders (nearly half of them) and so clearly commanded contemporary taste. It is without successors. It elaborates on nature, but incorporates its delicacy. These border tiles can only have been made with the most beautifully carved of stamps, cut in high relief with a patience exceeding even the artist's.

A swete suger lofe and sowre bayardys bun
Be sumdele lyke in form and shap –
                              (John Skelton, *c.* 1490)

Out of the Wessex school came the sweetest designing, clear-lined and uncluttered, literally the most memorable. Many individual designs are, in a sense, in a class beyond even Chertsey's and the harmonies of the Westminster pavement, because of their use and command of space. This command is seldom found among the Midlands and Penn designs, with exceptions like the design of three pricket or spiked candlesticks (of which there are examples in the St. Faith's Chapel of Westminster Abbey) and the rare merchant's mark at Chastleton in Oxfordshire (figures 37 and 38). Later on, the elegantly full designs of the Malvern revival achieved an effect totally different from the Wessex inlays. Something approaching the Wessex style reappeared only with Abbot Melton's sixteenth-century tiles at Hailes in Gloucestershire, which already had floors of thirteenth-century Wessex tiles.

Following on the first use of some uncomplicated mosaic shapes for the inlaid tiles at the Clarendon Palace in Wiltshire, usually only square tiles and rectangular border tiles were employed for inlays in the area labelled 'Wessex', after the kingdom of the West Saxons. These are tiles found mainly in Dorset, Somerset, Wiltshire and Hampshire. Some similar tiles in Oxfordshire and West Berkshire were called 'Wessex' by Christopher Hohler, but probably were Wessex-inspired and not Wessex-made. The positive use of space, through beautiful placing, that is made in these limited frames in some way suggests a commitment specially to tile-designing, separated from other media and, in particular, not owing as much to manuscript pictures and marginal ornamentation as the Chertsey tiles did. The inspiration of the Wessex subjects would be passed on to tilers in other areas – the designs *sumdele lyke in form and shap* – but not the special quality of openness. This openness was aided and typified by diagonal placing of the designs, which gained a line of nearly eight-and-a-half inches out of the six-inch square tiles.

113

38   MERCHANT'S MARK
Fifteenth-century inlaid tile, $4\frac{3}{4}$ inches square, at Chastleton Church, Oxfordshire.

MONOGRAM FOR ST. NICHOLAS
Stencilled initial and mitre, on later fifteenth-century screen panels at Castle Acre Church, Norfolk. Work similar to tile designing. (Original about $5\frac{1}{2}$ inches high.)

These Wessex tiles were made over a century and a half, from the mid-thirteenth century on. The first (partially surviving) were the tiles for Clarendon Palace, which are compared by Elizabeth Eames and Margaret Wood with the older tiles of the abbey church of Cunault in the Maine-and-Loire region of France. Late examples are tiles at Winchester College in Hampshire, bought for the college in 1412 at Newbury (Berkshire). The same designs with their variants were used throughout the period. Tile sizes, though, might be reduced and the designs might suffer a thickening or loss of stylishness. The classic examples belong to the thirteenth century. Tiles are usually large squares of six or six-and-three-quarter inches. They are also thick: the earlier, thicker ones are keyed with scoops of a trowel. The inlays are deep, but the glazes were seemingly less rich or pure and so less yellow than that used on the Westminster Abbey tiles or, much later, at Malvern. Worn surfaces are normal and look gently mottled. Plain black or dark green tiles (now worn) were a major feature, especially used for edging diamond panels, but there are also large and small inlaid rectangular border tiles – with designs such as fine foliage scrolls and pairs of castles or rosettes. Overall, these tiles form the most appealing group, but my pleasure and interest in their designs is somewhat anachronistic: the virtue and importance of individual designs is clear, but I do not know the region well enough and have not investigated enough tiles still *in situ*, whether in their correct 'divided' layouts or just in the mass. The older layouts were sometimes more elaborate than those of the inlaid pavements to the north, because of the retention of mosaic elements – but a number of them are known only from fragments or old plans. Such tiles were not made for a wide market, despite their numbers. Apart from Henry III's own tiles, most were laid at monastic sites, often at nunneries. These houses, however, were more often those of the lay-orientated Benedictines than of the Cistercians. Some abbey churches, of course, were made parochial after the Dissolution; others were abandoned, though a number of tiles might be salvaged then or later. I have missed out on full pavements and have seen proportionately too many loose examples in museums, examples that have retained clear designs but have lost most of their original colouring as well as their context. For the rest I may, consequently, have been over-impressed by the black-and-white certainties of the scaled-down illustrations in such literature as the articles by Knapp, Ward-Perkins and Stevens (see

115

the entries in the Booklist) and the *Royal Commission on Historic Monuments* volumes on Dorset.

The Wessex designs had an important rôle in establishing subjects for tiles, including the key subject of heraldry. Heraldry, in satisfying customers' demands, boosted the whole industry. At first the shields were those of owners and patrons only, as splendidly exemplified at Cleeve Abbey in Somerset, but then they were retained for general currency. What is particularly interesting in the adaptation (to tiles) of heraldic achievements or shields is that these were, so to say, patterns already. For tiles the colours were necessarily simplified, the shield shape itself was omitted almost as often as it was used and elaborations like crests and supporters were ignored. The first record of a grant of arms was made in 1127 by Henry III to Geoffrey of Anjou, but more shields were created only rather later and they became general for families with some land and status from the thirteenth century onwards when they coincided with the inlaying of tiles. The rules and French terminology were set in the thirteenth century. The rule that had most influence in tile-designing, and was very helpful, was that a metal – pale, whether gold or silver – should only be placed on or next to a colour. The colour provided a balancing dark ground or object, and in heraldry proper was usually red, blue, green or black. Whereas the Westminster pavement had the royal arms only, the Wessex sites have many different achievements. Geometrical charges were especially suitable for tile designs, but so were the lions – brave, stylish animals – which were favoured for shields from Geoffrey of Anjou's onwards. They relate well to the elegant mythological animals, most often griffins (the offspring of eagles and lions) and dragons, which are typical Wessex choices. They are often set in circles, with fleurs-de-lis in the spandrels. There was no difference in treatment; the bestiary is all equally real or unreal. The popular double-headed eagle design, the imperial arms of Richard of Cornwall as 'King of Almayne' (he died in 1272) was first used for tiles here; his English shield of a crowned rampant lion with a bezanty (gold coin) border was used on tiles in Wessex, but did not become one of the regular patterns.

An animal design that was created, and commonly used, in Wessex and gained permanent popularity was the 'birds-and-tree' pattern. This was of religious significance, with emblems of the Holy Ghost and the Virgin. The initial version had two long-tailed doves, addorsed but looking at each other, with a highly-stylised tree or fleur-de-lis between them. There are many variants. Other designs with foliage are typically formalised, the leaves seldom belonging to any particular plant, though there are some oak leaves and acorns like Chertsey's. 'Daisies' and 'rosettes' are used alone, like the pierced stars. Quadrants or four-tile sets are common, many forming foliate crosses out of four radiating fleurs-de-lis. Under the Penn regime these would descend into diaper-type patterns of comparative tweeness, similar to the little patterns seen on the cushions (head rests) in contemporary memorial brasses. The Wessex foliage scrolls form fluent arabesques, a stylisation nearly as great as that of the Renaissance foliage of the Lacock Abbey tiles of the mid-sixteenth century. Their lines are thin and twining, sometimes bearing small fleurs-de-lis instead of leaves.

Man-made items are also stylised. The simplified or stereotyped designs of castles are practically pictograms. They are often used in pairs and on border tiles, being typically Wessex, though the British Museum has Chertsey border tiles of about 1270 with castles. There are examples at many places, including Winchester Cathedral, but the design of a castle and rosettes – excavated at Amesbury Abbey in Wiltshire – is unusually crowded and unsuccessful. These castles came from the arms of Castile. Arcading was also employed: the Victoria & Albert Museum has examples from Keynsham and South Cadbury Abbeys in Somerset.

Despite the strong foreign influences, the creativity was both genuine and prolific. Dr. A. B. Emden has found 248 different designs in Dorset alone. Even what is lacking tells us something about good designing for floor tiles: comparatively niggling items like inscriptions and pictorial designs are seldom used. An exception is the combat of Richard I and Saladin, which is found in many places, but often incomplete and, in later versions, significantly inferior. Though Bindon Abbey (at Wool in Dorset) has classical border tiles with twisted chains, the dominant style for the beasts, the arabesques and foliage scrolls is oriental, perhaps immediately via France but, I think, previously filtered through Spain and its Moorish culture. The particular stylisation of the animals, especially the lions and the eastern griffins, and the setting of them in pairs or fours is most reminiscent of mediaeval textile designs, such as the twelfth-century silk brocade of the cathedral of Halberstadt, Regensburg, and various examples in the Victoria & Albert Museum. (See Archibald Christie's

I

Pattern Design, available in the Dover reprint.) Outstanding patterns, like Cornwall's spreadeagles at Sherborne Abbey and the very elaborate interlaces at Bindon Abbey, achieve uncrowded oriental complexity. We find real arabesques, involved repeating fretty (knots) and linked double boxes – rather like limners' decoration done with the pen – that demanded great skill of the stamp cutters.

There is a record that the 'whole' great hall of the royal castle at Winchester was to be paved in 1241 by 'Paulin Peyvere' and his assistant, and the dais was to be paved or re-paved in 1256. These tiles have disappeared, but the Clarendon excavations uncovered two pavements: that of the King's Chapel dated from 1244 and had circular (segmental) patterns with plain green dividers, while the Queen's Chamber pavement of 1252 consisted of six long panels, with square tiles bearing crosses, geometric designs and heraldry. The example of the later pavement was more influential, being followed notably at the royally-patronised abbey of Cleeve in Somerset. Clarendon designs are found elsewhere: one example is a four-fold grid pattern with trefoils, also used at Amesbury. (The Clarendon tiles were taken to the British Museum.)

Shaw in 1858 illustrated a large circular pavement at Great Bedwyn Church in Wiltshire, which is now reduced to museum examples. It was composed of 'square' slightly tapered tiles, inlaid with different fleurs-de-lis and oak leaves, with a diamond border. Related to this but more elaborate and also now lost, was a thirteenth-century pavement, over two hundred miles away, at Jervaulx Abbey in the North Riding of Yorkshire. Shaw could use drawings made in 1807 for the Marquis of Aylesbury, who removed virtually all the Jervaulx tiles to his collection. The layout included a huge wheel with radiating patterns. Individual designs belonged to the Wessex galaxy – birds, fleurs-de-lis, fretty, geometrical and heraldic patterns – and the plain squares that were also typically Wessex. Muchelney Church in Somerset fortunately has two circular pavements of segmental tiles, relaid from the Benedictine abbey. The designs, less ambitious, include foliage, fleurs-de-lis and cinquefoils.

Redistribution of tiles in this region has been common, though the totality is impressive. In 1860, for example, tiles with fifty-one different designs were dug up at the site of the Benedictine nunnery at Amesbury (Wiltshire) and were scattered between Salisbury's and other museums. Their designs were comparatively crowded, later

118

versions. There were pairs of birds, including small ones hanging from fleurs-de-lis like strange flowers. There was the face of a jack-of-the-green, also found in Winchester Cathedral, and heraldry including the lion of Cornwall and the three chevrons of Clare (with foliage in the spandrels). E. Keyte made tracings of them at the time, part of his large collection which is now in the Wiltshire Natural History and Archaeological Society's Museum at Devizes. Sites in Hampshire illustrate many of the uneven possibilities. Winchester Cathedral has the largest number of tiles, set in the three-aisled retro-choir, many worn, but including over sixty different designs most of which are thirteenth-century, five-and-a-half inches square and similar to Clarendon's. The area totals sixty-seven by eighty-three feet and includes a variety of groupings. Salisbury has about one hundred and fifty tiles only at the east end of the north aisle and more in the muniment room, but it is recorded that the whole of the cathedral was paved; the Chapter House tiles, with half-a-dozen designs only, are nineteenth-century replacements. Romsey Abbey has foliage quadrants with fleurs-de-lis *in situ*, besides rarer hunting scenes. Titchfield Abbey, a Department of the Environment ruin, has a mixture of tile finds: thirteenth-century Wessex animals and foliage; designs like those of the practically lost Chertsey-style pavements of the Worcestershire Premonstratensian abbey of Halesowen, which was the mother house; later mediaeval tiles, with hints of Wessex – such as pairs of little birds.

Dorset has some of the most attractive designs, but the pavements have suffered the same variety of fates. Shaftesbury has tiles in its abbey and in the museum. The Cistercian abbey of Bindon (Wool) has not been properly excavated and the site has been 'pillaged' in modern times, but it retains a nice range of relatively unambitious thirteenth- and fourteenth-century designs. Besides rosettes and foliage patterns, there are mythological creatures and heraldry, including the royal arms and Cornwall's eagle. A quadrant pattern with roundels is just like that at Clifton House in King's Lynn, Norfolk: is this mere coincidence or due to shared French influence? Sherborne Abbey has Wessex tiles on the retro-choir. Dr. Emden has rescued a fine and unique heron design, that was copied by Mintons (see Chapter 2). At Sherborne there are original tiles, laid diamond chequerwise in a group of four, so that they radiate outwards, with a marvellous design of a thin double-headed spreadeagle with its

CLIFTON HOUSE, KING'S LYNN, NORFOLK Detail of one of the two early fourteenth-century pavements. The tiles, which are $4\frac{3}{4}$ inches square, are set diamond-wise. The overall pattern is of bands and blocks of inlaid tiles, divided by bands of plain tiles. The circular design is a quadrant, needing four tiles to complete it. The design like rows of little battlements is heraldic, either 'embattled' or 'vair', the latter based on dark and light furs. Designs can still be made out, but the cracked and broken state of the tiles is similar to that of many church pavements (or their remains). The Clifton House tiles are notable both as a recent discovery with unusual designs, and as the earliest decorated tiles *in situ* in a secular site—a merchant's house.

tail feathers fanning out in a great triangle. This adaptation of Cornwall's arms was a notable response to the dictates of the square frame. Milton Abbas has two complex interlacing designs, which also needed a precise and patient stamp-carver as well as designer (or were they the same man?). These are reminiscent of Celtic manuscript ornament, but are wholly abstract and based on the square – like the classical key pattern. The Milton tiles were relaid in St. Catherine's Chapel in the nineteenth century: there are six hundred of them, from the thirteenth to the fifteenth century and with a great variety of designs – including post-Clarendon choices like armed horsemen,

120

dogs, stags and peacocks, a crowned Lombardic 'M' and the three birds of the see of Exeter.

Finally we should look at two important sites looked after by the Department of the Environment, where the early Wessex tiles have suffered contrasting fates. At Hailes Abbey at Stanway in Gloucestershire no tiles are visible *in situ*, though the site museum has examples recovered mainly from the nave of the church. Nave and presbytery were paved with tiles, many of them bearing the eagle of Richard, Earl of Cornwall, and the 'paly' for Sanchia of Provence, his second wife. Cornwall and Sanchia, a sister of Eleanor of Provence, queen to Henry III (elder brother of Richard), were buried in the abbey church. The 'paly' is a shield divided vertically into six 'pales' or strips, alternatively light and dark. The most recent excavations (1970s) have recovered more tiles from the site of the frater, or refectory.

Hailes was a Cistercian abbey, founded by Cornwall in 1246 after he had escaped from shipwreck in the Scillies. He endowed it with the parish church and manor of Hailes and an initial gift of 1,000 marks. (The mark equalled 13/4d.) The earl had great lands in southern England. Tiles of different dates and types have been found at Hailes, including Chertsey tiles, but the main groups are large and small thirteenth-century Wessex tiles, among which heraldry is dominant. There are still small tiles *in situ* underground, but three hundred of this sort (apparently moved there from the abbey) are in the parish church, which also has rare murals of about 1300 including Cornwall's heraldry, the castle of Castile and a winged elephant (irredeemably more frivolous than any of the Hailes tile designs). The tiles are set in the south porch (worn), inside the south door and in the chancel. Most are four-and-a-half inches square, but there are a few rectangular border tiles with a castle set between two fleurs-de-lis. There are designs with leaves, a fleur-de-lis in an oval fretty and the classic Christian fish symbol in an oval, but most of the designs are heraldic. They include the royals arms (in a circle), Cornwall's lion, Sanchia's paly, the three chevrons of Clare, vair in a diamond and a single-headed eagle – apparently also for Cornwall and done in two versions, one a rougher cut.

The colouring is interesting, even experimental. Besides yellow and near-orange glazes, there are greens which range from rich and dark to olive or blue-green – with the ground showing dark brown. On

121

some tiles the background, not the motif, is slip-coated, always un-usual.

The site collection (but the museum is being rearranged) has various heraldic designs: Castile; Provence; Old France, *semé-de-lis*, or sown or scattered with fleurs-de-lis; the English royal arms; Stafford; de Ferrers; Beauchamp; *gyronny* on a shield. Some of the shields record local patronage. The abbey gained great funds as a place of pilgrimage after 1270, when it was given a 'phial of the Holy Blood' and started a new building programme, which evidently disturbed some of the first pavements but added space for others. (See section (*e*) for the sixteenth-century tiles.)

The scene at Cleeve Abbey, at Old Cleeve (three miles south-west of Watchet) near Taunton, Somerset, is more coherent and aesthetically rewarding. The pavement of large tiles owes its survival to a monastic redevelopment. It is even treated with unusual respect in the official guidebook (by R. Gilyard-Beer). The bulk of the tiles are in the open air, on the old refectory site, so that they have to be covered over in the winter. They are uncovered at Easter. There are some more, re-set, in the chapter house. As at Hailes, there are further inlaid tiles in the parish church that probably came from the abbey. Cleeve was Cistercian, founded in 1198, but certainly expensively endowed in the thirteenth century by Richard of Cornwall, the builder of Launceston Castle, who confirmed the abbey's grant of Cornish estates. The old frater was erected in the late thirteenth century and its tiles date from between 1272, the year of Cornwall's death, and 1300. The new three-storey frater, adjacent, was built in the fifteenth century, when the smaller old frater was demolished and most of its tiles preserved by being earthed over. (Interestingly, a second floor room of the new frater-cum-dormitory has a mortar bed with the indents of lost tiles.) The old frater has a nineteenth-century composition of tile fragments to the dais, but most of the pavement of the body survives, little disturbed, and is laid out in three long and broad panels (east to west) with *inlaid* division tiles.

Heraldic designs dominate and among them especially the strong and simple geometrical arms of Clare, though the best known design is the fine, unfussy version of Richard I charging Saladin (on rectangular tiles). We find the three leopards of Henry III, the earlier version of the royals arms; the 'field' of fleurs-de-lis of Old France; Cornwall's lion in its bezanty border; his imperial eagle, here with streaked markings and rather clumsy heads; the chequerboard arms of Warenne or a local family, as at Hailes and Muchelney, with a castle above them and sycamore-type leaves in the spandrels.

The effective pattern of a foliate fleur-de-lis, set in radiating sets of four, was first used in the Queen's Chamber at Clarendon (1252) and was then employed in many Wessex pavements, including Keynsham Abbey's. At Cleeve, though, foliage is only a small element. It is used in the central panel with Cornwall's eagle and the Clare arms and in the north panel with the chequerboard shield. The most dramatic panel is on the south side of the old frater site, with sixteen-tile diamonds and half diamonds with the royal arms, the Clare chevrons and Cornwall's lion.

For the 'gules three chevronels or' of Clare the tile-designer reversed the colouring, leaving the inverted Vs dark (for gold) and slip-coating the ground (theoretically red). The powerful appeal of this shield may lie partly in its origins. The Clares, Earls of Gloucester, had great lands in the south-west, a marcher lordship along the Welsh border, besides estates in East Anglia – where the arms supplied a Bawsey relief design in the fourteenth century. This shield, however, would be a favourite in every district and period for inlaid tiles. The achievement was granted in the thirteenth century to Gilbert de Clare, who – explains Gerard Legh in the *Accedens of Armory*, 1562 – *builded iii greate houses in one province*. 'Chevron' was also the Anglo-French term for the paired roof timbers of a house. It owes its inspiring presence on tiles at Cleeve to the marriage of Cornwall's son Edmund to Margaret de Clare and, surely, to Clare benefactions.

(*c*) NORTH BANK AND MIDLANDS

It is rather churlish to link in one category the tiles of a region fanning out west and north-west of the comparatively uncreative London, and to group together later mediaeval tiles four to six inches square and inlaid or printed that are found from Buckinghamshire and Berkshire to Derbyshire and Nottingham. To do this is to include the known tileries round Penn (Buckinghamshire), Coventry, Droitwich, Nottingham and Dale and Repton in Derbyshire, besides postulated fourteenth-century kilns near Oxford and in Leicestershire and probably elsewhere. There is a cultural homogeneity justifying the grouping but, on the other hand, one cannot think of a region in which the systematic tile census will do more desirable and valuable work. (See the introduction to the Gazetteer.) In this region the pattern of the distribution of tiles has clearly been distorted by post-mediaeval industrial developments, favouring the by-passed country places – at least those which escaped Victorian improvements.

The region encompasses several different schools of tile-making, but with complex links that might possibly be disentangled into something like psychology's star and cluster diagrams of 'interpersonal relationships'. There are also links with other schools: the Wessex inlays influenced some designs found in Oxfordshire and Berkshire, while work done at Droitwich and Repton in the fourteenth century gave some inspiration to the slimmer but more closely packed motifs of the Malvern-style in the mid-fifteenth century. Echoes of thirteenth-century Wessex designs keep recurring, usually in smaller and thicker versions: the favourite addorsed pair of long-tailed birds with a stylised 'tree' between appears, outside Wessex, in places as far apart as Long Wittenham in Berkshire and Wirksworth in Derbyshire (the Wirksworth tiles are late nineteenth-century copies of the originals); a grid-like pattern of four small fleurs-de-lis reaches the church of St. Frideswide's Priory in Oxford (Christchurch Cathedral), is also used (for example) at East Shefford in Berkshire and becomes a very popular Penn design; the trefoil-knobbed fleur-de-lis in a circle, of which Long Wittenham has examples, goes right through the Midlands and Penn eras – only to reappear in a late version among the Malvern tiles (at Strensham in Worcestershire), with even narrower lines than the Wessex original.

Among fourteenth-century tiles west of the region we find tiles in different styles that are, however, easier to link with it than with Wessex. This is exemplified by the interesting but very fragmentary collection of tiles at Dilwyn Church in Herefordshire, which are set in the wall by the font and are white with damp. They are unusual in being six-inches square and perhaps as much as two inches thick, and some have reverse colouring – the design being dark and the depressed ground slip-coated. The bright tones, though, are those of Nottingham or Leicestershire; a very handsome fleur-de-lis, apart from its lily stamens, is particularly like a Derbyshire design; more surprisingly and coincidentally, a little stylised lion's head – with open mouth and wide eyes and spikes of hair between the ears – has close relations in the spandrels of Penn-style tiles. At Acton Burnell Church in Shropshire there are about nine hundred tiles, only four inches square, which are evidently older than, but rather like, the Penn-style tiles especially, out of the Thames Valley and Midlands group. The site is lonely, but the tiles must owe their presence to activities connected with the so-called Castle, an impressive fortified manor house of red sandstone (now in ruins). This was erected by Robert Burnell – Chancellor to Edward I from 1274 and the Bishop of Bath and Wells from 1275 – under licence to crenellate, granted in 1284. The tiles, many of which are very worn, are set in the north transept of the church. Some are green-glazed or self-coloured, but most are done in the group's normal colouring, similarly inlaid with unambitious geometrical-cum-foliage designs. There are recognisable oak leaves and more stylised leaves and 'flowers'. The date is suggested by a layman in fourteenth-century (or perhaps earlier) costume, set in a cusped quatrefoil, like the dragon design. The choice of such subjects as dragons and heraldic eagle could be linked with the oldest inlays, but these are done in the homely style which was to be favoured for mythological creatures in Nottingham, Warwickshire and the Thames basin. This treatment was partly the result of the small size. Most like Penn's are the repeating and quadrant designs, which make large and small circles and concave diamonds over a set of tiles.

Larger sizes were favoured by the monastic centres of Derbyshire and Droitwich and also for the earlier tiles in the west of the Thames Valley. These last were labelled by Christopher Hohler as 'Wessex', but they have heavier and simpler designs – of which the Ashmolean Museum has examples from Woodperry Church and Godstow Nunnery, near Oxford. They were to be superseded by the small Chilterns types, such as remain *in situ* in the muniment tower of New College, Oxford. The kind of tile which came to dominate the region was the convenient four-and-a-half or five inch square, fairly thin and made without keys, with an inlaid, or frequently printed, design. They were mass-produced, evidently often chosen from commercial stock. Plain division tiles were fairly uncommon. Mosaic disappears, except that, with the diamond layouts, triangular half tiles were needed to square off the edges of pavements. Figured tiles were used for this purpose. There is a similarity between all the tiles, for even the larger ones share in the decline in elegance which is compensated for by the wider range of subjects and a more naturalistic – or certainly less formal – treatment of some of those subjects. Foliate scrollwork is replaced by a dumpier battery of plants, while abstract arabesques vanish altogether. Fleurs-de-lis are thickened and multiply beyond counting: the tiniest versions, in the Penn tiles, punctuate pavements with the fertility of daisies. The select and alien fauna are invaded by new heraldic animals and by stags, rabbits and butterflies, as well as by monkeys and nameless grotesques – such as decorate the margins of contemporary manuscripts. The Midlands butterflies are spotted oddities, but the design problem of fitting a fully-antlered stag into a square was coped with well in the Midlands by giving them a semi-couchant position. Lions become puppylike. Man-made objects keep appearing, like candlesticks and crossed keys.

The increase in the number of armigerous families made its contribution to this provincialisation of style. The necessary multiplication of devices led to a more crowded heraldic geometry and to the introduction of such charges as corn stooks (garbs), mill irons (from the centre of a millstone, often in the form of the split-ended 'cross moline'), stag's heads and even hedgehogs. These developments coincided with the growth of the Midlands tile industry. The secular organisation of that industry obviously encouraged the choice of these shields for tile designs. Nottingham and Warwickshire especially favoured the use of the shield shape as well as the charges themselves. The repertoire included objects like bells and keys, as well as alpahabets in Lombardic scripts – sometimes mistakenly unreversed for 'printing'. All these motifs were also employed in Derbyshire. In the Midlands foliage was treated rather more naturalistically than it was by the Penn tilers, who tended to crowd together more simplified leaf and rosette forms – besides blurring the distinction between foliage and geometrical patterning. Oak leaves and acorns were popular.

Although it is not always easy to tell whether tiles were printed rather than inlaid and although a far higher proportion of mediaeval tiles must have been lost from the industrialised Midlands than from the Chilterns, it appears likely that the quicker method was developed in Nottingham or Warwickshire before it was used in Buckingham-shire. Late thirteenth-century printed tiles have been found, for example, in the Nuneaton kiln excavations.

Areas like Hertfordshire and Leicestershire gathered tiles or tilers from several different places. Many Hertfordshire, as well as Berkshire, churches have Penn designs; Hitchin's museum has tiles, found locally, which may have come from Leicester and are in the Nottingham style; Bengeo Church has Warwickshire as well as Penn designs. Leicester-shire is a veritable ragbag for tiles, apparently a catchment area in reverse, with Oxford, Penn, Midlands and Derbyshire designs. (Burton Lazars Hospital had its own kiln in the fifteenth century, which produced slip-coated relief tiles.) It is also difficult in a mixed county like Oxfordshire to make judgements about the originality and the source of designs. Chastleton on the Oxfordshire-Warwickshire border has tiles traditionally associated with Droitwich, but including Warwickshire designs – such as the holly leaves with berries, the six Boteler cups and the strange REWGW inscription (see Chapter 2), all shared with tiles at Bradgate House near Leicester (brought there from Ulverscroft Priory). We see the great William of Wykeham, Bishop of Winchester, of all people, contenting himself and his founda-tion of New College in about 1390 with four old printed Chilterns designs. These tiles are now special just because they have remained, undamaged, *in situ* in their panels. At the same date, though, under Wykeham's patronage the chapel of St. Cross Hospital beside

Winchester was paved with more original designs. In this region great abbeys like Reading and St. Albans acquired tiles of different dates and kinds, including Penn types, and seem normally not to have inspired or created their own designs.

On the other hand, a dose of patronage could produce good new designs. At Ewelme near Oxford, in the south (almshouse) chapel of the parish church, which was rebuilt when the almshouses were set up after 1436, are fine six-inch square heraldic tiles. These were evidently produced for Alice Chaucer, wife of William de la Pole, Chancellor of England, the co-founder. There were probably further tiles and designs in the body of the church as well: nearby Swyncombe Church, which has the lion design, has also two contemporary repetitive foliage designs, and Ewelme surely had also heraldry for de la Pole, including the family's three leopard's heads. What remain in the chapel are some punning wheels for Roet (for the name was the French word for wheel) with half a wheel on a step riser, and the splendid two-tailed lion design for Burghersh, the arms of Dame Alice's grandmother and her mother. Later in the fifteenth century some pleasant new designs, with a high mediaeval feel to them, appear in a few parish churches. Long Wittenham Church in Berkshire (sharing them with some Oxfordshire places) has examples, six inches square, with a nicely-organised oak-leaf pattern and a tile design relating to the Annunciation, which has a domestic jug for the usual lily pot and an illegible inscription in Black Letter.

The Penn-style tiles formed perhaps the most coherent group in the region. This commercial industry flourished, with the aid of Thames transport for its products, at places like Penn, Tyler's Green, Hedgerly and Burnham, in the fourteenth century. In the next century, evidently, the same designs were used for comparatively shoddy tiles made in or near London. Manufacture in this part of Buckinghamshire has left traces of kilns and also some contemporary documentation. Decorated tiles were supplied to grand addresses like Windsor Castle, the Black Prince's manor of Princes Risborough in Buckinghamshire (where some were found in excavations) and the Berkshire palace of the bishops of Salisbury at Sonning (Reading's museum has examples excavated at the site), as well as to the parish churches of large and small communities. Their distribution was neatly summarised by Ward-Perkins as 'chiefly in South Oxfordshire, South Buckinghamshire, East Berkshire and Hertfordshire'.

128

a, b, c

d, e, f

g, h, i

j, k

l

39   GEOMETRICAL AND FORMALISED FLOWER PATTERNS (*not to scale*)

(a) Wheel, St. Albans Abbey, Hertfordshire. (b) Wheel, single colour relief tile, found at Butley Priory, Suffolk. (c) Edelsborough Church, Buckinghamshire. (d) St. Albans Abbey. (e) Six-petalled flower, single-colour relief tile, Thetford Cluniac Priory, Norfolk. (f) Inlaid design for repeating patterns, Rievaulx Abbey and Mountgrace Priory, Yorkshire. (g) Flowers in broken fretty (interlace), Reading Museum. (h) Fretty, probably C 14 Nottingham tile, British Museum. (i) Acton Burnell Church, Shropshire.   PENN-STYLE QUADRANT TILES (j) Quatrefoil with trefoils; examples at Padworth Church, Berkshire. (k) Quatrefoil in roundel, with 'heads' in spandrels; examples at Blewbury Church, Berkshire. (l) Circular design from West Hendred Church, Berkshire, forming roundels and lozenges (tiles 4 inches square).

a, b

c

CIRCULAR DESIGNS

(a) Quadrant design with pears, late fifteenth century or sixteenth century, at Lacock Abbey, Wiltshire. (About 5 by 5¼ inches.)

(b) Early fourteenth-century quadrant tile with pale inlay in bluish ground, at Clifton House, King's Lynn, Norfolk. (Approximately 4¾ inches square.)

(c) Hexagonal tile (4¾ inches across) with rounded fret from Beaulieu Abbey, Hampshire, reproduced in Gough Nichols' *Examples*, 1845. An example of inlaid mosaic.

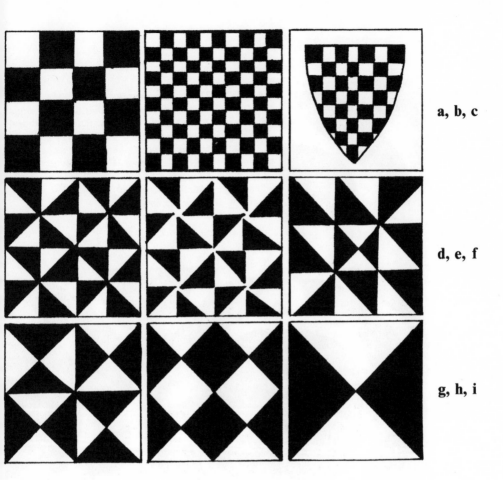

a, b, c

d, e, f

g, h, i

41   CHEQUERBOARD AND GYRONNY PATTERNS (*not to scale*)

(a) Butley Priory, Suffolk.
(b) C 14 tile, 6 inches square, West Hendred Church, Berkshire.
(c) 'Checky' shield (compare arms of Warenne), St. Albans Abbey, Hertfordshire.
(d) *Gyronny* pattern, common Penn-style tile.
(e) Tile with separate *gyrons* (triangles), Greyfriars Church, Reading, Berkshire.
(f) Variant of *gyronny*, Childrey Church, Berkshire.
(g) Cookham-on-Thames Church, Berkshire.
(h) Penn-style tile, London Museum.
(i) St. Albans Abbey.

131

42   GEOMETRICAL PATTERNING

The repetition and realignment of a single curved inlaid design makes an elaborate overall pattern, based on large and small 'circles', crosses and complex quatrefoils. The design is found at Broughton Church, Oxfordshire. Tiles $5\frac{1}{2}$ inches square. (*Repeat by Julia Ball, after a tracing by Dr A. B. Emden.*)

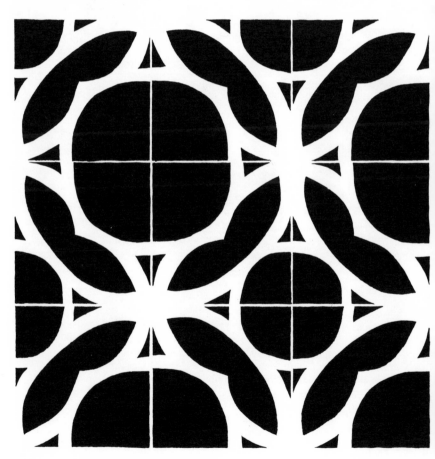

In 1352 (the accounts are printed in W. H. St. J. Hope's *Architectural History of Windsor Castle*, published in 1913) 65s. was paid for 10,000 tiles collected at Hedsor for the floor of the new chapter house in Windsor Castle complex. 4s. 2d. was paid to Elias 'Tilerer' and his assistant for five days' work in laying them. Later the same man set 8,000 tiles: paid *Elie tilere pro posicione. viij. ml. pavyng til in la fflor*. In 1362 and 1363 first 84,400 and then 11,000 more *pavementills* were brought from Penn. Some of the tiles that Elias is recorded as laying remain in the 'treasury' at Windsor. Documents seldom label clearly the type of tiles meant, but it is clear that the decorated ones were developed at Penn as part of an already established industry, which had long been making pottery, roof tiles and, presumably, plain floor tiles. As early as 1332 a tax return shows that three tilers at Penn had 15,000 tiles in stock between them. It also seems that roof tiles in the Penn area in the thirteenth century as well as the fourteenth century were sometimes partly glazed, making them more weather-resistant and also more expensive than ordinary roof tiles.

The relations between tile designers, tile-makers and 'paviours', or tile-layers, are not known, but a man like Elias obviously had numbered plans to follow for the layout or pattern of a whole floor. The Penn designs are relatively unambitious, so it is perhaps ironic that they include the rarity of a tile designer's signature. This design is found in several churches, for example Pitstone (Buckinghamshire) and Cookham-on-Thames (Berkshire). It carried the head of a lay-man, wearing a hood with a tapering end, and the Latin inscription RICARD' ME FECIT, 'Richard made me'. Pitstone, incidentally, has other inscriptions: AVE MARIA GRACIA PLENA, 'Hail Mary, full of grace', the opening words of the Annunciation, and the abbreviated SIGNUM SCĒ CRUCIS, 'the sign of the holy cross' with the letters set out in a cross – a design also known from St. Albans. Inscriptions, however, are uncommon among the Penn and closely related tiles.

Typically, Chilterns tiles are about four-and-a-half inches square, with unelaborate designs and fairly light yellowish colouring. They strike one has having a certain neatness, preferring regular foliage, flowers and simple geometry to more difficult subjects. In the corners, which have often suffered wear, there are leaves, rosettes or little faces or other devices, which act as links to extend the pattern. Though there is a design of three small shields and two leaves (excavated in London and at Hurley Priory in Berkshire, for example), the heraldic shields common in the Midlands are avoided. There are,

133

K

however, geometrical patterns covering the whole surface of the tile which were also popular for heraldry – and had been used before on Wessex tiles. Examples are 'checky' (or chequerboard), 'vair' (the undulating pattern based on furs) and *gyronny*, this often used for the tiles but exceptionally with separate triangles (*gyrons*) in the Reading Greyfriars Church.

Using comparatively simple elements, especially different shapes of leaves and circles, diamonds and quatrefoils, a great number of designs were made: the collection at St. Bride's Church in Fleet Street, London, includes over a hundred different patterns. Quadrants and radiating designs were preferred. An enormously popular repeating design was a quadrant with a fleur-de-lis in a diamond, with quarter circles in the spandrels. A common simpler motif was a flower with five rounded petals, sometimes set in a circle. Plain black and yellow division tiles were found when Hurley Priory was excavated in the 1930s, but in other places the patterns seem to have run on unchecked. They were about as routinised and adaptable as the offerings of the Victorian manufacturers.

Any birds and animals are usually subordinated to the other motifs. There are lions, for example, but most often they are reduced to heads grinning in the spandrels: they are debased versions of Wessex or Chertsey lions. Among the less common Penn and related designs are figures like the following, with some of their locations: hunting and hunted animals (examples at Reading Greyfriars and Notley Abbey, near Thame); a man on horseback, holding a hawk (examples found in London and at Hitcham church, Buckinghamshire); a man armed with a halberd (lost from Hurley, but not unique); mermaids with comb and mirror, of which Hitcham has two different versions; the head of a wild man or jack-of-the-green (worn example at Childrey, Berkshire); 'Holy Trinity' rabbits or hares, sharing three ears between them (Notley Abbey and Long Crendon, Buckinghamshire); the letter 'A' in Black Letter, probably for *Ave Maria* (found at Childrey and at Chilton Foliat in Wiltshire in a different surround).

There is no shortage of worn, or somewhat worn, examples of these Chilterns tiles: some churches still have considerable numbers of them, perhaps of two close types and dates, and not just fragmentary patches. A typical mixed group of tiles is that of Childrey Church, where there are about a hundred with geometrical and foliage designs, mostly, besides some plain yellow tiles: many are worn, but some pleasant individual designs emerge – especially oak leaves and some curly patterns involving rosettes. For their rare completeness, though, the fourteenth-century pavements of West Hendred, another isolated Berkshire church, deserve special attention. There are thousands of figured tiles, though with only half a dozen patterns, paving the chancel, the nave and the space by the font. They are set diamondwise. There are probably more under the pews, which are set on raised continuous boarding. The chancel tiles have been re-set in panels that are divided by modern plain tiles. They are four inches square, with two patterns only, both quadrants which complete small and large roundels. One is the top favourite, the fleur-de-lis with quarter circles; the other is an unusual purely geometric design based on two half circles. The fleur-de-lis tiles also cover most of the visible floor of the nave. Towards the west end and by the font there are six-inch square tiles, including plain yellow and green tiles. These bigger figured tiles also have geometrical and foliage patterns. One design has minute checks. Another is a quadrant design with acanthus-like leaves on a curved band (suggesting Paisley fabric), which is also found in a slightly smaller version at the disused church of East Shefford.

Although the total number of Thames Valley patterns is large, it seems probable that for many pavements only three or four different quadrants were chosen – to be repeated over and over again. It is intriguing to see the shift of emphasis in a design when it is used as a unit in a panel of its fellows – in other words when the correct layout survives. This is dramatically illustrated when the five-and-a-half inch square at Broughton (Oxfordshire) with a sophisticated abstract design is repeated, and pleasantly illustrated at Long Wittenham when oak leaf spandrels evolve into circular clusters of the leaves set round concave diamonds – on fifteenth-century six-inch squares. The shift occurs also, however, with the most ordinary Penn types. Cut in several slightly different versions is a popular mainly geometrical pattern with a strange little beady-eyed head in one corner – reminiscent of the wartime 'Chad' ('Wot no gasmasks!'), but without the nose. There are examples in the muniment tower of New College, Oxford, and in many churches, such as Blewbury and Cholsey in Berkshire. When laid *en masse*, quatrefoils are formed in one direction and in another the quartet of little heads surprisingly transforms itself into a dignified cross – a kind of 'cross paty', with wide ends. Repetition is not dull.

(*d*) MALVERN AND SEVERN

The inlaid tiles at, and traditionally associated with, the Benedictine church of Great Malvern in Worcestershire are some of the most rewarding to investigate. If without the excitement of pioneering work, they are sophisticated, harmonious and often delightfully coloured. Inscriptions, in Black Letter script, are frequent, well-organised and unusually legible. Belonging to the 1450s, the tile designs constitute a mature flowering, with inlays very shallow but clean-lined and exact. A few details, such as slit windows and cross-shaped *oeillets*, were incised in the pale slip of the special wall-tiles. Wear of the corners has rubbed out some of the foliage spandrels in particular, but the protective glaze was good. It gave most of Malvern's own tiles the glow of brown hen's eggs or conkers, but others have pinkish and mauve tones: these colours probably also owe something to the variety of colouring in the clay available here, for – despite the igneous pre-Cambrian outcrops looming over the town – this is a sandstone countryside. Stray survivors in the church at Little Malvern show that green as well as yellow was used for plain division tiles, and that the use of a paler than normal glaze on figured tiles produced a muted effect of off-white and a beiger brown ground.

The church of Great Malvern, with its stained glass and tiles, was saved by purchase by the townspeople after the Dissolution. (The same happened to Tewkesbury Abbey Church.) The chancel is paved with Victorian replicas, certainly made in Worcester, but about 1,200 of the originals were re-set in the curved wall of the reredos. Most are five-and-a-half or six inches square. There are as many as a hundred different designs. Both technical and artistic control are apparent, ensuring that harmony is the dominant quality in the tiles. The choice of subjects seems to have been conditioned as much by precise artistic ideas as by the demands of the religious and of high society. The main

136

categories are sacred emblems and inscriptions; stylised badges and heraldic achievements; foliage and flowers, often used to link tiles in sets. It is significant that figure and narrative tiles, as well as other old pictorial designs, are lacking – although there are hints of naturalism in the drawing of the typical, carefully-organised vine and hawthorn leaves, the roses and the daisies. The irregular lines of more representational designs would have interrupted the formal pattern-making.

The unifying decorative factors included the controlled use of the same elements both as a main design and as a small part of a design, for example the much repeated crowned IHC monogram for Christ, the crowned double 'M' for the Virgin (the second M lying below the first, reversed like a reflection in water) and the instruments of the Passion. Both the instruments of the Passion and the bleeding heart emblem are placed in shields, just like the secular heraldry. Cusped borders and octofoils relate different designs to each other, and quadrant tiles complete circular foliage bands and multiply the other patterns. There is a closeness between the shapes of the crowns, the thin knobbed pinnacles (a foliate derivation, regularised Flamboyant) and the foliage contained in spandrels or daggers (*mouchettes*).

The architectural motifs, especially the pinnacles, remind us more of things seen in painted glass than in other tiles. Way, in *The Gentleman's Magazine* in 1844, described them as 'ornaments comfortable to the style of architecture or character of decoration prevalent at the period, but devoid of any special import', and this still seems to identify both their formality and their feeling of *lateness*. The pattern-making is clever. It is interestingly demonstrated by the treatment of some apparently intractable machinery, a portcullis: by a very good design adaptation or absorption this (with its side chains) is placed across the corner of a quadrant tile and is given at its base only a single heavy arrow-head, which threatens the opposite spandrel and the centre. A wide curved 'V' (inscribed) below echoes the arrow shape, but also links the adjoining tiles to form a central quatrefoil. The portcullis was probably included as the badge of the Beauforts. Stretton Sugwas Church in Herefordshire has good, little worn examples of this design.

Exact dates are given to the tiles at Malvern by inscriptions on the fine (repeated) sets of rectangular tiles. These read *anno d'm. cccc. liij*, A.D. 1453, and *anno r. r. h. vi. xxxvi*, in the 36th. year of the reign of king Henry VI, that is 1457/8. They share motifs with the other tiles, but were most unusual in that they were made as wall tiles, to be set in panels round the high altar. Rearrangement, loss to museums and total loss have only partly dissipated their force. An ascending set of five tiles, each measuring eight-and-a-half by six-and-a-quarter inches, is like a narrow section of a very intricate building – whose traceried windows, overhanging jetties, bridges or canopies and pinnacles with crockets (projections) take up more space than the emblems. At the base is a tree with the nest of a pelican, wounding its breast to feed three young; then there is a shield of the English royal arms quartered with the French fleurs-de-lis; then the crowned monogram IHC; then, over two elaborate windows and a roof line, a shield of the instruments of the Passion with the spear and the ladder at the sides; finally, their tips interrupting the modest Henry VI dateline, there is a dense group of dreaming pinnacles. Gough Nichols in 1845 illustrated four tiles from a fairly simple cross made of five or six tiles, which would also have been more effective set on a wall, but I think these have disappeared. The Ashmolean Museum in Oxford has an ambitious larger tile, of nine by five-and-seven-eighths inches, which is supposed to have come from Great Malvern. This has the same pierced architectural frame, with crocketted pinnacles, and a large foliate crown over the main design: this is the haloed figure of the Resurrected Christ, thick and Germanic-looking, but rising from the tomb in the classic mediaeval Italian pose with wounded hands displayed. His chest is slashed almost into the bleeding heart emblem. The perspective between tomb and floor is not handled with success, but interestingly this floor consists of alternate dark and light tiles.

The greatest loss at Malvern itself is the layout of the pavements, though the many four-tile sets are obvious. The survivals at Little Malvern and the example of other related floors indicate that plain dividers were also used – reducing the likely over-intensity *en masse* of numerous different close-lined designs and bringing out the overall patterning. The greatest elaboration is seen in a miniature circular or rose window design. The dark and light of a real, and by then old-fashioned, curvilinear window was reversed, the pale inlay representing the tracery and the dark ground the variously-shaped lights. The main plan may be seen as circles set between the five points of a central star, but the groupings are elusive, with 'hourglass' and 'Y' or swallow-tailed butterfly forms appearing and dissolving between the circles or lobes. Perhaps only the gentleness of the Malvern

RESURRECTION TILE Mid fifteenth-century tile probably from Great Malvern, with design showing the Resurrection of Christ, classically posed, stepping out of the tomb. This is one of a set of wall tiles, the tile size being 9 by $5\frac{7}{8}$ inches.

colouring makes this flickering window tolerable on such a tiny scale. (See plate IV. Rosettes and pairs of leaves in the spandrels have suffered wear.) By contrast, a more traditional and effective spareness is seen in the design of cusp-finned fish on a pointed oval. This was an emblem for Christ: this same design was used among the contemporary (lost) tiles of Worcester Cathedral and is very like an older Wessex version in Hailes church in Gloucestershire. Other designs that are full but uncrowded and particularly successful are the sacred monograms; the *mentem sanctam* inscribed tile with its big central rosette; much of the heraldry, more especially the badges; a thin trefoil-ended fleur-de-lis (of the 'tree' form) set in a circle and with the elegance of an early printer's mark, of which there are good examples at nearby Strensham; and two foliage-dagger designs, shaped like exotic toy windmills. Apart from the fleur-de-lis, which is a much refined version of a favourite Wessex design, these are all without close stylistic precedents.

Some idea should be given of the range of the heraldic designs, from the royal arms and those of connected families of national importance to those of local status only – for example the Braci, holders of the nearby manor of Madresfield, who figure as donors in the window glass. As with the heraldry of the Penn tiles, though, arms were also used just for their decorative value in pavements throughout a wide region. The royal shield of three lions is set in four-tile groups, with the inscription *fiat voluntar* (or *voluntas*) *dei* – let God's will be done – and in the corners facing pairs of strangely-elongated birds (with pin heads and very long tails). The six birds (martlets) and cross of Edward the Confessor or of Westminster Abbey appears. So does the double-headed eagle of Cornwall, set in a circular border studded with bezant coins. On further shields are the six rampant lions of Bohun; the three chevrons of Clare, much favoured for tiles of all dates; the Despenser fretty (angular knots); the different crosslets of Beauchamp of Warwick and Berkeley of Berkeley, Gloucestershire. The local Braci arms of two spur rowels and a cross bar appear in a circle on genuine quadrant tiles, alternating with a shield which 'impales' (halves) Braci with an 'engrailed' or wavy cross. The badges include the wheel hub and knot of Stafford; the punning talbot dog, labelled 'Sir John Talbot', also found in the Canynges' pavement; the swan of Bohun, which makes a particularly attractive pattern. In the nineteenth century the rebus (punning badge) of Tydeman de Winchcomb,

Bishop of Worcester (died 1401), was recorded here and at Worcester, but apparently no example survives: the design consisted of a bishop's mitre above a wool *comb* and a *winch* (capstan), around which a rope is coiled or *tied*. Some of these arms and devices, thus, add man-made objects to the Malvern repertoire, but most of the arms of the great old families are geometrical. They also bring in a few pre-selected animals, paradoxically making us realise that these designers normally preferred foliage and flower heads to fauna: they neglected such established subjects as stags, hunting dogs, king's heads, knights-on-horseback, dragons and grotesques, besides ordinary geometrical patterns. Theirs was a specialised as well as creative revival of fine tile-making. The formal flowers and leaves they marshalled with tapestry-style denseness, benefiting from the now comparatively large span of six inches.

The bulk of the inscriptions are in Latin, some with the abbreviations familiar from documents and from memorial brasses. With a shield of the Passion, for example, appears a prayer, *pax Cri. int. nos sit semp. amē*, for *Pax Christi inter nos sit semper*, *amen*, the peace of Christ be among us always. They were interpreted with antiquarian enthusiasm in the nineteenth century. The usually clear letters are set out on strips or bands, sometimes just making a border to the tile, sometimes organised into complex patterns in which the order of the words becomes unclear. They can have been intended for the truly literate only. A four-tile repeat invokes the Evangelists – *Marc, Mathe, Lucas, Joh – miseremini mei, miseremini mei, saltem vos amici me quia manus dni (domini) tetegit me,* 'have pity upon me, have pity upon me, at least you my friends for the hand of God has touched me, A.D. 1456'. More enigmatic is the invocation, *mentem sanctam, spontaneum honorem deo, et patrie liberacionem* – a holy mind, honour free(ly given) to God and liberty to the country. This is known also on tiles found at Nottingham, Shrewsbury and York and was recorded also in Holy Trinity Church at Stratford-on-Avon. The words were the prayer and epitaph of the tortured St. Agatha, martyred in Sicily in the third century, later used as a charm against fire. G. C. Dunning, in an article on inscribed jugs (in *Mediaeval Archeaology*, 1967) relates this charm to various other deciphered and undeciphered pieces of verbal witchcraft favoured in the Midlands region. In the newly-respectable vernacular is the so-called 'executor's tile' found also at Little Malvern, York and (lost) Stratford-on-Avon. It reads like a wordly-wise extension of the many *memento mori* inscriptions which were especially popular for memorials in the later Middle Ages, threatening the living with the abruptness of death and the awfulness of decay. From the mid-fifteenth century the use of English, replacing Latin, was generally on the increase. This is an eight-line poem, inlaid on a tile without any relieving decoration. The idea is that a man should carry out his wishes in his lifetime, for:

> *Think, man, that thy life may not ever endure,*
> *That thou doest of thyself of that thou art sure;*
> *But that thou keepest unto executors' care,*
> *And ever it avail thee, it is but aventure*

(or a matter of chance). The original reads:

THENKE. MON. YI. LIFFE

MAI. NOT EŪ. ENDURE.

YAT. YOW. DOST. YI. SELF

OF. YAT. YOW. ART. SURE.

BUT. YAT. YOW. KEPIST

VN. TO. YI. SECTUR. CURE.

AND. EŪ. HIT. AVAILE. YE.

HIT. IS. BUT. AVENTURE.

How many manufacturing centres supplied the area over which Malvern-style tiles are distributed is unknown. One guesses that the great Benedictine monasteries, at places like Gloucester, Tewkesbury, Worcester and, most probably, Evesham had their own kilns. Evesham's tiles are reduced to a collection of stray finds (kept in the Almonry building), but these are significantly of different dates and types, the latest including the Malvern-style crowned 'M'. A commercial kiln or kilns for decorated tiles, such as had long been organised in the Midlands, seems the likely arrangement for the great port of Bristol. All the centres are likely to have supplied numerous parish churches in their own vicinity. The hundred different designs remaining at Malvern suggest this place had the primacy in design-making, but it is easier then to believe in tilers travelling with design stamps than in thousands of tiles *often* being transported many miles. It seems probable, though, that Great Malvern supplied little places like its neighbouring house of Little Malvern and Strensham (Worcestershire) and Stretton Sugwas (Herefordshire). Strensham's is a small, unrestored and isolated church, whose nave retains numbers of heraldic, flower and foliage tiles – their inlays often clear despite the loss of glaze. Malvern most likely supplied the Hospital (or almshouse) of Ledbury (Herefordshire) with its tiles: the chapel there has sixteen- as well as four-tile groups. The Malvern-type tiles found as far to the north as St. Mary's Abbey in York have been connected with the Repton kiln (Derbyshire). These are kept in the Yorkshire Museum, in the same park as the abbey ruins.

If Leominster Priory – where the church has fragmentary remains of Malvern quadrants – made its own tiles, it could also have supplied the parish church of Croft, to the north-west, which retains good tiles. (Both are in Herefordshire.) Whether these came from Malvern or from Worcester or elsewhere in the Severn valley, there are Malvern-style tiles in a fair number of Worcestershire churches. Worcester itself has unfortunately lost the tiles (in the cathedral's 'Singing School') that were there to be recorded by Henry Shaw for publication in 1858. This floor had the exact Malvern mix of foliage and heraldry.

Tewkesbury Abbey, which has a fair number of Malvern-style tiles and has evidently lost many more, houses a perfect microcosm of the student's world of tiles, exemplary uneven riches: it could provide both an irresistible introduction to the subject of inlaid tiles and a perfect training ground. After mosaic, start here. There are modern replicas in the choir. The mediaeval tiles – in every state from excellent down to fragmented or erased – remain or have been re-laid in a collection of tiny places round the choir. There are worn remnants of pavements in the famous chantry chapels of Edward le Despenser (erected between 1390 and 1400), of Robert Fitzhamon (about 1395) and of Richard Beauchamp of Warwick (after 1422). The last has the best examples, later in date than the chapel, perhaps, and including plain brown and yellow tiles. There are inlaid tiles in a recess in the south transept and in two recesses on the south side of the ambulatory. Loose tiles are gathered in museum cases in the south-east chapel of the ambulatory. There is a range of types: earlier four-inch squares, carrying lions, fleurs-de-lis and so on; the classic birds-and-tree design on a five-inch square; six-inch square Malvern designs, including the IHC inscription, window tracery, bears on two-tile sets, pairs of facing peacocks (or is this design of different provenance?), vine and oak leaves and daisies. As for the reproductions, 'the floor

143

of the choir is paved with tiles made in 1879, which are careful copies of mediaeval tiles found in various parts of the eastern portion of the Abbey' (D. W. Maclagan). These mediaeval tiles were excavated from 1875 to 1879. There are many different designs, most in, or related to, the Malvern-style. The tiles are laid diamondwise in groups of four, twelve or sixteen, with black divisions between. Notably there is a sixteen-tile group which has lions, with flowers between their teeth, crawling round a circle – as in original tiles surviving in Broadwas Church (Worcestershire). There is a similar large pattern of muzzled bears, with one bear to two tiles, – perhaps connected with the bear and ragged staff badge of Beauchamp of Warwick. These lions and bears are of the fifteenth century, but were not used at Malvern. The rectangular tiles of castles (for Castile), double-headed eagles and lions – reminiscent of the borders in fourteenth-century glass windows in Herefordshire – are earlier Wessex designs. Malvern supplied designs such as the Clare and Berkeley arms, inscriptions, 'wheels', flowers and foliage. It seems likely, from the old and new evidence, that several pavements with new and fashionable designs were laid in the abbey in the first half of the fifteenth century, but that some older sections were allowed to remain.

To the south there are some Malvern or Severn tiles in Dorset as well as Somerset (Dr. A. B. Emden). The most important groups, though, are those in St. David's Cathedral in Pembrokeshire and the high altar pavement in Gloucester Cathedral. The St. David's tiles pave the approach to the high altar in the presbytery, the top step having been repaired by Gilbert Scott. The total area is about thirty square feet. The tiles are slightly smaller than Malvern's own, like those of the Canynges' pavement from Bristol with which it shares some sets. A sixteen-tile group has foliage and daisies centering on a rose. The heraldic designs include the arms of Berkeley. St. David's was run by a secular college, not by a monastic order. This fact alone – at this time of Benedictine artistic dominance in the region – might suggest that these tiles were 'imports' from Malvern. Geology and geography, though, provide more compelling reasons for believing that they were brought by sea – probably from Bristol. There are some similar tiles in the parish church of Carew, near Tenby, to the south-east. Carew also has rectangular heraldic tiles, of six-and-a-half by four-and-a-half inches, including the arms of St. David's and of Sir Rhys ap Thomas, late fifteenth-century holder of the thirteenth-century castle from which they were brought in the nineteenth century.

The Gloucester pavement redresses Malvern's major loss, for the tiles retain their proper layout. This was a special commission, involving the making of original designs, for Abbot Thomas Sebrok. One tile gives the exact date, 1455. Nine tiles are needed for the four-fold circular dedicatory inscription. Plain 'black' tiles are used between the panels, the tiles being set diamondwise. Besides inscriptions, there are heraldic and foliage designs in the Malvern style. A special feature is the fine repeated design of window tracery. This has two circular-headed lights to a tile (set square), and is of fourteenth- rather than fifteenth-century inspiration.

There are now firm plans for the display of the uprooted Canynges' pavement in the British Museum. It has been the subject of detailed study (see the article by Elizabeth Eames, *Journal of the British Archaeological Association*, XIV, 1951). Its original location was in the first floor solar or parlour of the house of William Canynges, near the magnificent church of St. Mary Redcliffe in Bristol. Bristol, then second only to London in size, was the main port for the West of England, Wales and the Midlands. This Canynges was its greatest merchant and shipowner; supplier of ships used for the renewed campaigns against France; twice member of Parliament; five times mayor; perfector of St. Mary Redcliffe; employer, according to William of Worcester in 1478, of eight hundred seamen and a hundred workers in the building trades; and credited with the largest ships – he had one of nine hundred tons when between two hundred and four hundred was usual for merchant vessels – and the 'farthest commerce' of England. For all this, interestingly enough, the pavement shows signs of economy. This could be explained by its having been organised, hurriedly, for a visit in 1461 by Edward IV, as Mrs. Eames suggests. The source of the designs, if not of the tiles, was Malvern. They are secular patterns.

The tiles were 'lifted' in 1913, when a number were lost. (Canynges' house was demolished in 1937. Despite this I think it unfortunate that Bristol does not have the tiles.) Their condition was good because they had been protected by a later wood floor. The 654 tiles extant reached the British Museum from the Rutland collection: they are enough to pave an area seventeen feet by ten feet nine inches. They include plain dark tiles, used to frame the four- and sixteen-tile diamond panels of figured tiles. They are slightly smaller than Malvern's.

145

There are duplicate or near duplicate designs, such as the rose and leaves and the inscribed badge of Sir John Talbot – but here with 'Talbott' instead of 'Talbot'. Some of the designs are taken from cut-down stamps, but the Confessor arms come from a stamp with the birds incorrectly reversed. The colouring is rather duller than Malvern's, attributed by Mrs. Eames to overhard firing, and the glaze was comparatively patchy. The record of the pavement in Shaw's book (1858) shows that there was always some inconsistency in the layout, again suggesting that the tiles were bought from stock rather than specially made.

The designs chosen were of heraldry, animals and formal foliage, especially vine leaves and tendrils. The lion with the flower in its mouth is close to the Broadwas design (see Tewkesbury above). The sixteen-tile group with the vine-patterned circle is shared with Malvern, but has its own extras – grapes as well as leaves, besides small dragons in the spandrels. This set has its own interesting internal economy, for only three designs were needed. In fact the vine design was also reversed, unnecessarily and spoiling the alternating pattern of leaf and grapes. Oddities, not found at Malvern, but used in more than one design in the Canynges' pavement, are the spotted heart shapes.

The punning talbot dog badge was a suitable choice for Canynges, since Sir John was a military leader in the French wars while the merchant supplied ships. Talbot was killed in 1453 at the battle of Castillon, Dordogne. It seems surprising that a man with Canynges' resources resisted having his own merchant's mark – which appears several times on his tomb-chest in St. Mary Redcliffe – made into a tile design. If these tiles were chosen like a ceramic carpet, with attractive designs but little personal reference, and if the 1461 dating is correct, the reason is probably that Canynges was nearing the end of his long career. His wife had died in 1460 and he himself in 1467, aged 67 or 68, would take orders and retire to his charitable college of Westbury as its dean.

It is a pity that no tiles were made with the merchant's mark, practical but enigmatic like most of these devices, to balance the more elaborate emblems of status based on fighting and lands. Merchants' marks were very frequently used on buildings and in glass, recording great financial contributions, and on tombs and brasses. Feering Church in Essex even has a moulded brick example in the vaulting of the south porch. They are, despite the attractive stray example at Chastleton (Warwickshire), oddly absent from mediaeval tile design. Set diagonally across the tile, this conventional sign could have made a good tile motif, probably with Malvern leaves and flower heads round it.

(*e*) SIXTEENTH-CENTURY INLAYS

The tile scene in the first half of the sixteenth century was characterised by some scattered revivals of fine inlaid work, for which the main motivation was heraldic. This applied both to the ecclesiastical customers – before the Dissolution – and to secular customers. New designs were made to order, including the initials, rebuses (punning emblems), badges or coats-of-arms of the patrons. After the Dissolution the redistribution of property gave a boost to secular demand, for the newly-prosperous grantees or purchasers of monastic property would convert or build anew and mark their buildings with their arms – carved over stone archways, painted or plastered on ceilings and perhaps inlaid in a tile pavement, though surviving tiles are few. The styling of the designs might be traditional, like those which included the (old) Russell arms of a chevron and three rosettes, laid at Chenies, the Buckinghamshire mansion of John Lord Russell. John Williams of Thame, Treasurer of the Court of Augmentations – which disposed of the monastic lands – had some quite ordinary new tiles made for himself. These had heraldic designs, among others,

147

and were laid in the chapel of Rycote House (removed to the successor house) and in the chapel of Thame Park, his Oxfordshire acquisitions. Since Henry VIII and Wolsey had long before turned to imported tiles, these two rich courtiers were being conservative in their choices, but by now the Reformation had increased cultural nationalism.

At least as early as the 1520s more inspired designs had been made for Abbot Melton of Hailes in Gloucestershire. Close to these were the 'good' inlaid tiles discovered at the Blackfriars site in Gloucester, their heraldic motifs showing they were first made for the nearby Augustinian house, Llanthony Priory. The most modern tiles, however, would be the product of the Renaissance. These were Sharrington's delicate, Italianate tiles, made for his ex-monastic property of Lacock Abbey in Wiltshire.

Traditional tiles that were, nevertheless, designed with considerable panache are the large heraldic tiles from the unfinished Thornbury Castle in Gloucestershire. (They reached the Victoria & Albert Museum in the 1890s.) Done in a detailed but quite thick inlay are the royal arms and those of Edward Stafford, Duke of Buckingham, both with antelope supporters and encircled by the ribbon of the Order of the Garter, and the badges of Stafford and other great families close to the throne. The royal arms are done on a panel of four tiles. The badges include the chained swan of Bohun (used by Henry V and successive monarchs), the flaming wheelhub of Buckingham and the Stafford knot. Some of these devices were moulded on the tall brick chimneys of Thornbury, one of which carries the date 1514. The heraldic boast was significant and dangerous: in 1521 Henry VIII had Stafford, who was his Lord Constable, tried for treason and executed – as a magnate too close to the succession and with a private army of retainers of the style long ago banned by Henry VII. Thornbury, a mansion not a castle proper, was started in 1511. We have, thus, both an exact period and a fraught political context for the tiles. It was pointed out by Arthur Lane that the cusped form of the shields was 'the only essentially non-Gothic detail' on the tiles, but the script of the Garter motto is also unorthodox – definitely not the time-hallowed, less-legible Black Letter. These designs are both strong and stylish, rather than elegant. One regrets the museum cases.

The Melton tiles are unfortunately divided between the fragmentary display at Hailes Abbey itself, the British Museum, and other places. Hailes Abbey, a Cistercian house in Gloucestershire, had inlaid tiles

43 LATER MEDIAEVAL TILES WITH LETTER 'A' INLAID, PROBABLY FOR 'AVE MARIA' (HAIL MARY) *Left* Tile 4¾ inches square, from Chilton Foliat Church, Wiltshire, reproduced in *Specimens of Tile Pavements* by Henry Shaw, 1858. *Right* Simplified version, with letter 'A' in circle, in south transept chapel (dedicated to the Virgin) of Childrey Church, Berkshire. (Approximately 5 inches square.)

LEAF AND FRETTY DESIGNS WITH THE INSCRIPTION 'RM' FOR 'REGINA MARIA' (MARY AS QUEEN OF HEAVEN). Fourteenth-century tiles, about 4½ inches square, at Harpsden Church, Oxfordshire. (Adapted from Shaw's *Specimens*, 1858.)

149

L

44   WALL TILE DATED 1457/8, WITH ARCHI-
TECTURAL MOTIFS AND LETTERS 'IHC' (FOR JESUS,
DERIVED FROM THE GREEK FORM).
One of a set of five ascending designs at Great
Malvern Priory Church, Worcestershire. (About
$6\frac{1}{4}$ by $8\frac{1}{2}$ inches.)

GROUP OF FOUR TILES, OF BETWEEN 1511 AND 1521, FROM THORNBURY CASTLE, GLOU-
CESTERSHIRE (Victoria and Albert Museum).
The inlay shows the arms of Edward Stafford, Duke of Buckingham, with the Order
of the Garter inscribed 'HONI SOIT QUI MAL Y PENSE', and Buckingham's heraldic
badges—including the Bohun (and royal) swan and the Stafford knot. (Tiles $6\frac{3}{4}$
inches square—a corner of one tile is slightly chipped.)

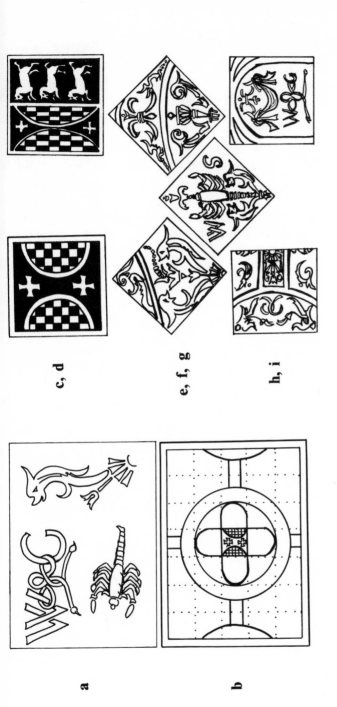

c, d

e, f, g

h, i

a

b

45   RENAISSANCE TILES OF ABOUT 1550 AT LACOCK ABBEY, WILTSHIRE. Tile pavement of Sir William Sharrington, with his arms and initials and those of his third wife, Grace Faringden, his scorpion badge and Renaissance motifs. (a) *Details* Initials 'w' and 'G' linked by knot; scorpion; dolphin (*not to scale*). (b) Plan of section of pavement (24 tiles) centering on Sharrington's arms. (The layout was recorded by J. A. Gotch about 1900). Five Renaissance designs form linked roundels and sets of four. The tiles are 5 inches square. (c) Arms of Sharrington (shield omitted). (d) Arms of Sharrington 'impaling' arms of Faringden – with three unicorns. (e) to (i) Renaissance designs used for the roundels – (f) and (i) have initials, and (f) includes the scorpion badge, laid in radiating sets of four. (All tiles 5 inches square.)

of several styles and periods, notably heraldic tiles of the thirteenth century. Anthony Melton was abbot there from 1509 to 1527, displaying in his tile commissioning at least the sort of luxurious egotism seen in Prior Vyntoner's contemporary lodgings at St. Osyth's in Essex. The tiles (five-and-seven-eighths inches square) have designs of a striking new elegance. On one the royal arms are fitted round a complex foliate shape, but Melton – lacking personal heraldry – has his name spelled out beside an abbot's mitre and crozier or is represented by a punning tun (wine barrel). Designs without rebuses are a lively, stylised pair of birds (with a joint collar) and a counter-charged fleur-de-lis, with ground and inlay reversed down the centre. Interestingly, this very attractive and rare parti-coloured design has a simpler predecessor among the small thirteenth-century tiles now in Hailes parish church. A tiny discrepancy in the sixteenth-century fleur-de-lis pattern leaves one with the query, was this accidental – perhaps the stamp carver's mistake – or intended to give a touch of lightness? The brown cusped border has three dots at a point where the yellow inlay opposite forms a trefoil. (In some versions the original rounded tip of the fleur-de-lis has been cut away into a cusped shape, but the rest of the design remains unaltered. See figure 5. The change takes away a likeness to the eagle's tail – see below.)

Since the Hailes site has been so pillaged it is perhaps fortunate that two hundred and fifty of Melton's tiles – at an unknown date – reached the Huddlestons' old manor house of Southam de la Bere, near Cheltenham. There they were once more relaid by Lord Ellenborough, eldest son of Lord Chief Justice Ellenborough (who died in 1818). In 1845 Gough Nichols, author of the *Examples of Decorative Tiles*, recorded that this was done 'some years ago'. The tiles, with the quadrants correctly laid in their radiating sets of four, were used to pave a small room off the great hall. There they remained, comparatively unknown (and latterly covered) until they were taken up early in 1974: the intention is to use them in the decoration of the new country club at Southam. Their original location may have been the Chapter House at Hailes.

To see these tiles in the mass is to realise, with admiration, how technically consistent they are and how original and effective are the numerous diagonally-placed designs. Most are worn, but tiles from the edges of the room have suffered little more than loss of glaze – which was evidently clear rather than rich (that is, not very yellow). The five-and-seven-eighths inch squares are pretty consistent, with a thickness of about one-and-one-eighth inch and a slight bevel, but no mortar keys. Surfaces are very flat and smooth; the inlays are shallow, but very precise. Melton's tiles look like a revival and swan-song of English tile designing, though there are some Renaissance elements. Inventiveness is shown in the use of parti-colouring – for the fleur-de-lis, the two-headed eagle, a rose with buds – and of small dark inset figures and of reverse colouring. The crowned lion of Richard of Cornwall, in its shield with a bezanty (coin) border, is done in light on dark and in dark on light. Melton also revived the arms of Richard as Emperor; the eagle, which had been employed on thirteenth-century tiles laid near the founder's burial place. The re-cast eagle is a most striking design (see figure 25).

Melton perhaps used the Beaufort portcullis badge as a compliment to Lady Margaret, mother of Henry VII. Truly modern designs, though, are the double rose of the Tudors and the exotic pomegranate with its bulging seeds. Both, especially a beautiful rose in a wreath design, are strongly reminiscent of embroidery – though the pome-granate was carved for courtier Sandys on fine panelling at the Vyne in Hampshire. This fruit was the emblem of the Spanish princess, Katherine of Aragon, married to Henry VIII in 1509. Melton's crozier is a tiny ecclesiastical item among these lovely secular patterns.

Lacock Abbey, near Chippenham (Wiltshire), is open to the public from April to October (National Trust). It consists of the remains of a thirteenth-century nunnery, around which was built for Sir William Sharrington, the mid-sixteenth-century purchaser, a fashionable stone mansion. Sharrington, an associate of Lord Protector Somerset, was notable as an early patron of the Renaissance style – and as a fraudulent treasurer of the Bristol mint. The tile pavement is full of pure Renaissance motifs. Some two hundred of the tiles survive at Lacock, and there are some examples in the Victoria & Albert Museum. (Illustrations appeared in J. A. Gotch's *Early Renaissance Architecture in England*, 1901, and in an article by Frank Stevens in the *Wiltshire Archaeological Magazine*, volume XLVII, 1935–37.) They are full – perhaps overfull – of bases, garland-like drapery, stylised foliage, stylised dolphins and Sharrington's apt scorpion badge. They centred on his arms and the unicorn arms of his third wife (Grace Faringden) and their initials are included in the designs. Most of the tiles are quadrants, which formed radiating sets

153

of four dolphins, while sixteen tiles made up a wreath of foliage. The inlay is very fine and precise, and the colouring of the glaze is a soft olivey-yellow. Though they were the product of a detailed English commission, these are sophisticated, elaborate, un-English tiles – no revival but practically beyond our subject.

Short gazetteer of mosaic and figured tiles

This list mainly comprises tiles at – or supposedly still at – their original sites, although they may have been relaid or kept loose. Some museum collections are also included, the British Museum and the Victoria & Albert Museum having specially large collections of different types of tiles. It would have been prohibitive in time and money to check by visits, or even letters, whether all the places mentioned even in this short list still have their tiles, so I must apologise if any are found to have disappeared. At the state-administered sites tiles still *in situ* may be covered over, for their protection, during the winter months. When tiles have gone from their original location it is worth looking for them in the local museum or the county museum. I have seen many of the places listed, but to have confined the gazetteer to these would have made it quite unrepresentative. It has seemed the lesser evil to include other places derived simply from printed sources, old and new.

It is always worth searching a parish church or cathedral for mediaeval tiles. The examples may be few and elusive but pleasant, like the single rampant lion at Aldworth in Berkshire or an owl remaining, with an otherwise rather pathetic collection set in the steps down to the crypt, at Madley Church in Herefordshire. Nineteenth-century pavements may include copies of the original tiles. At places with monastic connections the tiles are often particularly interesting, even if not numerous, for the range of decorative methods they show. This is as true of small places like Sawtry in Huntingdonshire or Elstow in Bedfordshire as it is of a great cathedral like St. Albans or the great ruined abbey of Rievaulx in the North Riding.

Eventually illustrated lists of the surviving decorated tiles, set out by county, will become available through the auspices of the British Academy and the Society of Antiquaries. This tile census has been initiated by Dr. A. B. Emden and organised by Mrs. E. S. Eames.

The local Government Act which came into force in 1974 *altered a number of county names and boundaries. For convenience, this Gazetteer gives the new identification in brackets if a change has taken place.*

SCOTLAND

EDINBURGH

National Museum of Antiquities   Relief tile finds from the C 13 kiln site at North Berwick Abbey (East Lothian); mosaic tiles from Cistercian houses; square tiles from Glenluce, etc.
Royal Scottish Museum

ROXBURGHSHIRE

Melrose Abbey   C 13 mosaic tiling *in situ*. Similar to Byland's (Yorkshire). Dark and pale interlocking tiles, including fleur-de-lis layout. Individual patterned tiles, too, both impressed and inlaid. Site museum has loose tiles from here and from Newbattle Abbey in Midlothian, also Cistercian. (State-administered.)

WIGTOWNSHIRE

Glenluce Abbey   Cistercian. Square inlaid tiles survive in Chapter House and elsewhere. (State-administered.)

WALES

CARMARTHENSHIRE (DYFED)
Kidwelly Castle   Inlaid tiles. (State-administered.)

GLAMORGAN

Neath Abbey (West Glamorgan)   Cistercian. Later mediaeval tiles of West Country or Severn type. Designs mostly heraldic. (State-administered.)

MONMOUTHSHIRE

Tintern Abbey (Gwent)   Cistercian. Chapter House has some simple, straight-sided mosaic, probably C12. Inlaid heraldic tiles have been removed. (State-administered.)

PEMBROKESHIRE (DYFED)
Carew Church   Two types of heraldic tiles.

St. David's Cathedral   Pavement of mid C 15 Great Malvern style tiles, including foliage and flower patterns.

ENGLAND

St. Bride's Church (Fleet Street)   In crypt are displayed later mediaeval Penn-style tiles: nothing dramatic, but over a hundred different designs.

Westminster Abbey   (1) St. Faith's Chapel has some Penn-style tiles. (2) The octagonal Chapter House has marvellous panelled floor of Chertsey-style tiles of 1253–59: no mosaic, but some 4-tile groups and rectangular border tiles.

British Museum   (1) In public gallery until recently have been displayed groups of mediaeval tiles of all styles and dates, including C 13 deeply inlaid Wessex tiles, Chertsey tiles and C 14 Penn types. Also Tring 'Apocryphal Infancy'. (2) In the collection but not to be displayed until end of 1974 the 17 × 10 ft Canynges' pavement of about 1450, from Bristol, and mosaic pavements from Byland and Rievaulx. Examples of the different types to be redisplayed then.

London Museum   The *Medieval Catalogue* written mainly by J. B. Ward-Perkins, has 81 drawings illustrating the bulk of the collection, tiles found in the London area and either locally-made or derived from Penn and other kilns in the Chilterns. There are both inlaid and stamped tiles, typical – pleasant rather than exciting – furnishing of ecclesiastical and secular buildings in a populous south-east district. Mostly foliage and geometrical designs.

Victoria & Albert Museum   The English tiles (Room 141) are very much part of European collection described in the *Guide to Tiles* by Arthur Lane. Examples of all types, including Rievaulx mosaic, Chertsey, Wessex and Great Malvern inlaid tiles. Early Tudor tiles from Thornbury Castle, Gloucestershire.

Old Warden Abbey   Excavation in early 1960s uncovered Cistercian mosaic pavement, with overall geometric pattern but including such individual designs as five-pointed stars and a rose with fleur-de-lis. Now re-covered.

Willington Church   Mixture of tiles (see Chapter 2).

Childrey Church (Oxfordshire) Bucks-type tiles, mostly in N transept. Very worn, but wide range of designs including *gyronny*, fretty, foliage, the letter 'A' and a (worn) 'wildman's' head.

Cholsey Church (Oxfordshire).

Cookham-on-Thames Church About 300 tiles of different dates, supposedly from Burnham, Bucks.

East Shefford Church C 14 tiles, including some complex patterns.

Long Wittenham Church (Oxfordshire) Patches of tiles, including 14 with 4 Wessex-derived designs.

Reading (1) *Museum*: Some tiles on display, including some from Benedictine Abbey (and many more abbey tiles in store). (2) *Greyfriars Church* (Friar Street): Some animal tiles (Bucks.), reset in mortar slab.

Remenham Church

Stanford Dingley Church Unique C14 brick-shaped tiles, with inlaid designs on two faces.

West Hendred Church (Oxfordshire) *Thousands* of C 14 tiles, 4- and 6-inches square, with recurring patterns, foliage and fleurs-de-lis.

Chalfont St. Giles Church

Chenies Manor House R.C.H.M. cited C 16 tiles in hall (and contemporary heraldic glass). Chenies is an Early Tudor brick house, erected by John Russell: 4 inlaid tiles form shield of Russell arms, chevron between three rosettes.

Chesham Bois Church

Edelsborough Church

Great Missenden Church

Hitcham Church

Horsenden Church

Lillingstone Dayrell Church In chancel C 13 embossed tiles and also C 14 slip tiles.

Little Kimble Church C 13 Chertsey tiles (Tristram and Isolde).

Little Missenden Church

Long Crendon Church C 14 tiles in sanctuary, including 'Holy Trinity rabbits' design.

Monks Risborough Church

Netley Abbey (near Long Crendon) (Private house.) Variety of tiles of C 14 and later, including hunting scenes.

Pitstone Church   Chancel has C 14 and C 15 Penn-style tiles. Some unusual designs and inscriptions, including the tiler's RICARD ME FECIT (Richard made me) design – known from other places too.
Saunderton Church
Thornborough Church   C 15 tiles in nave and N aisle. Many worn.

For details and for other Buckinghamshire tiles see the *Royal Commission on Historical Monuments* volumes (published in 1913), which indexed over 30 locations – mainly with Penn-style tiles.

CAMBRIDGESHIRE

Ely   (1) *Cathedral*: S transept has some tiles. (2) *Prior Crauden's Chapel:* This detached building (S of cathedral) has complete tile pavement of about 1325. Mainly mosaic, with some line-impressed and inlaid tiles. Also irregular mosaic 'Temptation' scene panel. (See Chapter 4, section *c*.)

CHESHIRE

Audlem Church
Birkenhead, Williamson Art Gallery (Merseyside)   Tiles from Birkenhead Priory in collection. (Others in museum at Chester.)
Chester   (1) *Chester Cathedral*: A few re-set tiles in N choir aisle. (2) *Grosvenor Museum*: Large number of tiles in collection, mainly from Chester itself and including the cathedral.
Church Lawton Church
Eastham Church (Merseyside)
Goostrey Church
Great Budworth Church
Malpas Church
Norton Priory (Runcorn)   Mosaic tiles at site of Augustinian house recently excavated.
Woodchurch Church (Merseyside)

DERBYSHIRE

Ashbourne Church
Bakewell Church
Dale Abbey   Unable to check survival of C14 tiles, but British Museum has examples.
Morley Church   About 200 tiles, from Dale Abbey tilery. Designs 'most attractive': heraldic, foliage and animals, geometric.

159

DEVONSHIRE

Buckland-in-the-Moor Church   Small inlaid tiles.

Haccombe Chapel   Over 600 C 14 inlaid tiles, including heraldic and religious designs.

DORSET

Milton Abbas, St. Catherine's Chapel   In C 19, tiles in good condition were transferred from site of Benedictine abbey to this surviving chapel. Inlaid tiles of C 13 to C 15 (see *R.C.H.M.* vol. III, pt. 2). Great variety of designs, including frets and interlaces.

Shaftesbury   (1) *Abbey*: Some tiles remain in ruins of this important Benedictine nunnery. (2) *Museum*: C 13 and C 14 Wessex tiles, the 'better preserved' ones, from *Abbey*. (British Museum also has some.)

Sherborne Abbey Church   Church of Benedictine abbey has large number of Wessex tiles in retro-choir.

Tarrant Rawston Church

Winterbourne Abbas Church

Wool, Bindon Abbey   C 13 and C 14 Wessex-style tiles in choir and refectory of ruined Cistercian abbey. Designs include foliage and heraldry.

For other Dorset tiles see the *Royal Commission on Historical Monuments* volumes (apart from one volume, all published in 1970s).

ESSEX

Alphamstone Church   C 14 tiles in chancel.

Colchester Castle Museum

Great Bentley Church

Great Oakley Church

Harlow Church

Hatfield Broad Oak Church

Inworth Church

Leez Priory   (Private House.) C 14 heraldic tiles found during excavations.

Little Oakley Church

Norton Mandeville Church

Saffron Walden Museum   Inlaid tiles from local churches.

West Thurrock Church

160

Bristol (Avon) *The Lord Mayor's Chapel*   Poyntz Chantry has re-set mediaeval English and C 16 polychrome Spanish tiles.
Buckland Church   C 15 tiles.
Gloucester Cathedral   1455 Malvern-style pavement in front of high altar, with ecclesiastical and heraldic designs.
Hailes Abbey (Stanway)   Fragmentary survivals of fine inlaid tiles from C 13 Chertsey and Wessex types to C 15 and C 16, in site museum. (State-administered.)
Hailes Church   Tiles from *Abbey*, mainly heraldic designs and foliage types. Colours green as well as yellow.
Newland Church   Some Malvern-style tiles.
Southam de la Bere   Fine early C16 tiles that were designed for Abbot Melton of Hailes now re-laid (in the Country Club).
Tewkesbury Abbey Church   Victorian copies of C 15 Malvern-style tiles and some late mediaeval originals.
Winchcombe Church   Tiles, in 2 frames, from lost abbey.

HAMPSHIRE
Beaulieu Abbey   Displays of fine tiles from thirteenth-century Cistercian abbey, including inlaid mosaic.
Romsey Abbey Church   C 14 Wessex inlaid tiles.
Titchfield Abbey   Inlaid tiles.
Winchester   (1) *St. Cross Almshouse Chapel:* Tiles of 1390, some with motto 'Have Mynde' (or take spiritual care).
(2) *Winchester Cathedral:* Over 5,000 late Wessex tiles in retro-choir, including heraldic tiles. Described by A. Clifton-Taylor as 'the largest surviving expanse' of 'normal' mediaeval church floor. (Articles in *Winchester Cathedral Record* by Emden, 1948, and Knapp, 1956.)
Yateley Church   Chilterns-style tiles.

HEREFORDSHIRE (HEREFORD AND WORCESTER)
Abbey Dore Church   A few C 13 tiles, some with relief fleur-de-lis and some with heraldic inlay.
Brampton Bryan Church
Croft Church
Dilwyn Church   Very worn C 14 tiles by font.

Ledbury, St. Katherine's Hospital C 15 Malvern heraldic tiles in mediaeval chapel.

Leominster Priory Church Survivals of different types, mainly C 14 but with some C 15 Malvern-style tiles. Heraldry and foliage. Some tiles 12 ins. square. (At W end.)

Madley Church C 14 tile fragments in crypt steps.

Stretton Sugwas Church Malvern tiles in vestry.

HERTFORDSHIRE

Aldbury Church Penn tiles.

Flanuden Church

Hitchin Museum Collection of local and Nottingham-style tiles.

King's Langley Church C 14 Penn tiles.

Meesden Church Early C 14 mosaic pavement with circular plan. Yellow and green tiles, some with inlaid designs.

St. Albans (1) *Abbey*: Scattered survivals of all dates and types, from C 13 relief to late foliage and animal designs.

(2) *City Museum*: Tiles from *Abbey* and *Sandridge*.

Sandridge Church Penn tiles.

Sarrat Church

HUNTINGDONSHIRE (CAMBRIDGESHIRE)

Sawtry Church C 13 and C 14 tile survivals from lost Cistercian abbey, a cell of *Old Warden Abbey* (Bedfordshire). Range of types: plain or *mosaic*, line-impressed, inlaid. Black and green tiles.

KENT

Bekersden Church Tiles, some of C 13, from Lesnes Abbey, Erith; 'It is known that the abbey tile-works were at Bekersden' – Ronald Jessup (*Kent,* 1950 ed. of *Little Guide*).

Brook Church Considerable numbers of mediaeval tiles.

Canterbury Cathedral Hundreds of tiles, of different dates, mainly in Wax Chamber, Treasury, Eastern Crypt.

Harbledon Church Mediaeval tiles in nave.

Stone Church C 15 tiles, including foliage patterns.

LEICESTERSHIRE

Belvoir Priory

Bradgate House Tiles in chapel of ruined house. Worn, but large number of different designs.
Cossington Church
Croxton Abbey
Leicester (1) *Abbey.*
(2) *All Saints' Church.*
(3) *Museum.*
Melton Mowbray Church
Ulverscroft Priory Numerous tiles of C 14 and C 15, including heraldic designs. Scattered patches *in situ*, but most kept in house museum.

LINCOLNSHIRE
Revesby Church (Lindsey) Small part of C 13 mosaic pavement from Cistercian abbey site. Star forms set out in bands. Colours: black, yellow, green.
Thornton Abbey, Lindsey (Humberside) Some tiles. (State-administered.)

MIDDLESEX (GREATER LONDON)
Ruislip Church (St. Martin's) C 14 tiles in chancel, designs including foliage and heraldry.

NORFOLK
Barton Bendish Church Tiles in sanctuary.
Castle Acre Priory Remains of pavements of Bawsey tiles and plain single colour tiles. An inscribed tile (in site museum) asks for prayers for the soul of Nicholas of Stowe, Vicar of Snettisham, who died in 1376. (State-administered.)
Castle Rising Castle 300 Bawsey relief tiles re-set over a fireplace. Most designs heraldic. Bawsey tiles also found in recent excavations. (State-administered.)
King's Lynn (1) *Clifton House*: Two tiled floors of about 1325, belonging to a mediaeval merchant's house. Inlaid designs, including knight on horseback, lions, fleurs-de-lis and yellow circles on blue ground. Oldest secular tiled floors, discovered ten years ago.
(2) *Museum*: Tiles of different types, including Bawsey relief tiles.
North Barningham (or *Barningham Norwood*) *Church* Rare mosaic of tile and stone, forming wheel or rose-window.

163

Norwich (1) *Castle Museum*: Tiles, including Bawsey relief tiles, from East Anglian sites.

(2) *St. Peter Hungate Museum*: Tiles from various sites, including Castle Acre and Castle Rising. Bawsey relief heraldic, animal and geometrical patterns.

Rougham Church A few Bawsey relief tiles, set inside the tower.

Thetford Cluniac Priory C 14 relief tiles survive, though worn, in choir of ruined church and in infirmary chapel. Some heraldic designs.

NORTHAMPTONSHIRE
Harrington Church
Higham Ferrers Church
Northampton Museum Tiles including Penn types.

NOTTINGHAMSHIRE
Nottingham Castle Museum Mediaeval tiles from several areas.

OXFORDSHIRE
Brightwell Baldwin Church
Broughton Castle The chapel has C 14 tiles.
Charlton-on-Otmoor Church Penn-type tiles. Designs mostly geometrical, but also some small animals.
Chastleton Church C 14 inlaid tiles, including sets. Heraldry and foliage.
Ewelme Church Numerous tiles recording, through their heraldry, the founders, William de la Pole and his wife (Alice Chaucer). Designs include Roet wheel & Burghersh two-tailed lion. C 15.
Goring Church Mostly C 13 tiles surviving from Augustinian convent, with bird, animal and foliage designs and the double-headed eagle of the patron, Richard of Cornwall.
Oxford (1) *Ashmolean Museum*
(2) *Christchurch Cathedral*: Firstly priory church, then reprieved as college chapel and cathedral of new diocese (1540s). Despite changes it retains many mediaeval fittings, including very small remnants of decorated paving. These are C14 Penn-and-district style tiles (e.g. 4-fold fleur-de-lis). At pillar bases, etc., in E part of church.
(3) *Merton College*: Mediaeval in Library, amazingly laid in 1620s.
(4) *New College*: Muniment Tower has complete floor of C 14 Penn-

164

style tiles with four designs only, set diamond-wise.
Stanton St. John Church   Batches of C 14 inlaid tiles, with two repeating fleur-de-lis designs.
Thame Park Chapel

SHROPSHIRE (SALOP)
Acton Burnell Church   (Neighboured by C 14 Bishop's Palace.) About 900 small inlaid tiles in N transept, apparently C 14, many very worn. Many geometrical patterns, with flowers and foliage, man in C 14 costume, eagle, dragon, wyvern.
Cound Church
Haughmond Abbey   State-owned. Some tiles.
Stokesay Castle   Tiles from church laid in an upper room. They are small, very worn, with inlaid designs including fleur-de-lis, daisies, 'vair' (heraldic representation of two-colour fur), lion, dog, stag, whirlygig.

SOMERSET
Cleeve Abbey   (Old Cleeve) Several other patches of tiles survive, but the best group is the Frater (Refectory) pavement dated, by its heraldry, between 1272 and 1300. Special emphasis given to double-headed eagle of Richard of Cornwall, a benefactor; the three leopards of Henry III; the three chevronels (inverted 'V's) of powerful Clare family. Other heraldic tiles and foliage designs. Richard I and Saladin charge each other. These are all deeply inlaid Wessex-type tiles, set diamond-wise. (State-administered.)
Glastonbury Abbey   Wessex tiles, mainly 4-tile sets, in site museum. Designs geometrical and heraldic. (State-administered.)
Luccombe Church
Muchelney Church   Two circular mosaic pavements with inlaid designs, from suppressed abbey. Wessex-style and of C 13. Designs include foliage, fleurs-de-lis, cinquefoils.
Watchet Church (Near Cleeve Abbey.)   Many tiles in chancel.

STAFFORDSHIRE
Hanley Museum, Stoke-on-Trent. Potteries exhibits, including mediaeval tile collection.
Tamworth Museum

165

Butley Priory (Near Woodbridge.) The tiles then excavated were recorded by J. N. L. Myres in *Archaeological Journal,* vol. XC, in 1933. He found mainly C 13 & C 14 relief tiles, detecting foreign influences in them. Designs, some rare, including fret (knot), birds with 'tree', wheel and foliage-tailed lion. These apparently survive, not *in situ.* (Priory not open to public.)

Denston Church

Great Wenham Church

Icklingham All Saints Church Redundant church near Bury St. Edmunds. In chancel C 14 mosaic tiles in style of Prior Crauden's at Ely, but extra shapes and more line-impressed designs – such as pinnacles and faces. (Information, Hallam Ashley.)

Lakenheath Church

Leiston Abbey In 1363 canons moved here from earlier site, probably bringing floor tiles with them. These include embossed tiles like Butley's. Some heraldry. (State-administered.)

Westhorpe Church

SURREY

Chertsey Museum No tiles remain at site of Benedictine Abbey, but some rich chestnut and yellow survivors are distributed between this new museum and others (B.M., V. & A., Guildford). Variety of forms derived from mosaic, but with finely inlaid designs. These include heraldry and scenes from the Tristram and Isolde 'romance'.

Guildford Museum Collection has tiles from Chertsey Abbey, Waverley Abbey (Cistercian) and some Surrey churches. The Chertsey tiles include mosaic and figured roundels (some from Tristram story).

SUSSEX

Etchingham Church (East Sussex) 1363 building has decorated floor tiles. Especially good animal designs, including deer and hunting dog.

WARWICKSHIRE

Coventry Art Gallery (West Midlands) Second World War raids uncovered a mediaeval tile kiln and tiles. Among tiles displayed, some heraldic designs.

166

Nuneaton, St. Mary's Priory Church   Fragments of tile pavement of the Wheel of Fortune.
Wormleighton Church

Devizes Museum   Museum of Wiltshire Archaeological Society. Has Wessex tiles from several sites including Great Bedwyn Church (where no tiles now remain).
Lacock Abbey   Some C 13 tiles in old sacristy of Augustinian nunnery; Renaissance tiles of between 1540 and 1553 made for the lay owner Sir William Sharrington after the Dissolution, with dolphins and Italianate foliage. (National Trust; open to public.)
Salisbury   (1) *Cathedral*: Some remains of Wessex tile paving (for example, at E end of N aisle), but the early C 13 pavement of the Chapter House was replaced by a copy about 1870.
(2) *Museum*: Tiles include some from the site of Clarendon Palace, of the time of Henry III. (More examples in British Museum.)

Bredon Church (Hereford and Worcester)   C 14 tiles from Droitwich, mainly heraldic.
Broadwas Church (Hereford and Worcester)   Droitwich or Malvern tiles, including heraldic.
Cotheridge Church   Malvern-style tiles including arms of Gloucester Abbey and the inscribed 'executor's tile' (also found at Great Malvern).
Evesham, The Almonry Museum (Hereford and Worcester)   Different types of tiles from the Benedictine abbey. Most C 14 heraldic or geometric design. A few later and more elaborate, including a Malvern-type crowned 'M' for Virgin Mary.
Fladbury Church (Hereford and Worcester)   Heraldic tiles, including arms of Berkeley and lion and black bull badge of Edward IV.
Great Malvern Priory Church (Hereford and Worcester)   About 900 decorated tiles, with fine quality inlaid designs, survive in church of Benedictine priory. Some are rectangular wall tiles, inscribed for Henry VI in the mid C 15. Designs include sacred letters such as 'IHC' for Christ; window tracery and pinnacles; vine and foliage patterns and daisies. Much heraldry, including arms of Clare, Despenser, Beauchamp. Warm brown ground due to rich yellow glaze, but

167

also some pinkish or mauvish tiles. The Benedictines' tile kiln was found nearby in 1833. They mostly supplied the Severn Valley region, from parish churches to Gloucester Cathedral.

Holt Church (Hereford and Worcester)   C 15 tiles include ones with the talbot dog badge of Sir John Talbot (also found in the Canynges' pavement from Bristol, now in British Museum) and Latin-inscribed *misere* (pity) prayer tiles.

Little Malvern Priory Church (Hereford and Worcester)   Worn tiles in chancel, heraldry predominating but many other Malvern designs. Roundels. Foliage. Some inscribed.

Redditch (Hereford and Worcester)   (1) *Bordesley Abbey* (Tardebigge): There are records of tiles and tile-house (kiln) being sold after the Dissolution, but recent excavations have uncovered $4\frac{1}{2}$ in. square figured tiles.

(2) *St. Stephen's Church* (Church Green): In Victorian times a C 14 tile pavement from *Bordesley Abbey* was laid in the vestry. Tiles of different sizes and shapes which suggest, despite the designs being inlaid, the continuing influence of Cistercian mosaic.

Shelsey Walsh Church (Hereford and Worcester)   C 15 tiles in chancel, including sets of 12 or 16. Malvern-type.

Strensham Church (Hereford and Worcester)   Isolated church has brasses, C 15 painted panels and a nave floor of C 15 Malvern tiles, the designs mostly found also at Malvern itself. Inscriptions; heraldry; lions; birds; roses and daisies; oak and sycamore leaves; fleur-de-lis.

YORKSHIRE

Byland Abbey (North Yorkshire)   Cistercian abbey. Mosaic paving of C 12 or early C 13 remains, chiefly pavements of 2 S transept chapels. Largest area of mosaic *in situ*. Many different shapes, with diamonds in majority. Colours are greens, greys and yellow. (State-administered.)

Fountains Abbey (North Yorkshire)   Cistercian. Mosaic remains. (State-administered.)

Jervaulx Abbey (North Yorkshire)   Cistercian. No mosaic, but the inlaid tiles (many removed in C 19) were laid to form radiating pattern.

Meaux Abbey, Wawne (Humberside) Cistercian. Ministry of Public Building & Works excavated kiln site by North Grange Farm.

Rievaulx Abbey (North Yorkshire)   Cistercian abbey. Early mosaic tiling, like Byland's, the main colours grey and yellow. Also some C 14 tiles, either plain squares or inlaid with fleur-de-lis, flowers and geometrical patterns. (State-administered.)

York   (1) *The Yorkshire Museum*: Collection includes early embossed tiles; C 14 inlays; C 15 tiles of Repton or Malvern type from neighbouring St. Mary's Abbey (Benedictine).

(2) *York Minster*: Tiles in Chapter House.

Booklist

This booklist includes the main general texts, now rather old, and articles on the more notable examples of mediaeval tile manufacture. It should be supplemented by articles on regional types or on individual sites published in the county archaeological magazines, particularly for East Anglia, the whole South Coast and its hinterland and for the West Country. Tiles are sometimes mentioned or briefly described in the Royal Commission on Historic Monuments county volumes (see indexes) and in the Nikolaus Pevsner *Buildings of England* series published by Penguins. Useful lists of buildings with tiles *in situ* were given in the introductory sections of some of the *Little Guides* series, now out of print.

AME, EMILE. *Les Carrelages Emaillés du Moyen-Age et de la Renaissance,* Paris, 1859. (Many block illustrations. Part I is a general history of pavings. Part II concentrates on the later mediaeval inlaid tiles of the Département of Yonne, SW of Paris.)

BARNARD, JULIAN. *Victorian Ceramic Tiles,* Studio Vista, 1972.

BORENIUS, TANCRED, and CHARLTON, JOHN. 'Clarendon Palace: An Interim Report', article on the Wiltshire site in *The Antiquaries' Journal,* XVI, 1936.

CHATWIN, P. B. 'The Mediaeval Patterned Tiles of Warwickshire', article in *Transactions and Proceedings of the Birmingham Archaeological Society,* LX, 1936.

CLAYTON, P. T. B. 'The inlaid tiles of Westminster', article in *Archaeological Journal,* LXIX, 1912.

CLIFTON-TAYLOR, ALEC. *The Pattern of English Building,* 1962, (& revised edition published by Faber & Faber 1972).

CROSSLEY, F. H. *English Church Craftsmanship,* Batsford, 1941, (section ix, on 'Decorated Floor Tiles').

DAVEY, NORMAN. *A History of Building Materials,* 1961. (The tile pavement cited for Ely Cathedral, however, does not exist.)

EAMES, ELIZABETH S. *Medieval Tiles – A Handbook,* (British Museum), 1968.

'The Canynges Pavement' (from Bristol, now in the British Museum), article in *Journal of the British Archaeological Association,* XIV, 1951.

'The products of a mediaeval tile kiln at Bawsey, King's Lynn', article in *The Antiquaries' Journal,* XXXV, 1955.

'A Thirteenth-century Tile Kiln Site at North Grange, Meaux, Beverley', article in *Mediaeval Archaeology,* V, 1961.

'A Thirteenth-century tiled Pavement from the King's Chapel, Clarendon Palace', article in *Journal of the British Archaeological Association,* XXVI, 1963.

'A Tile Pavement from the Queen's Chamber, Clarendon Palace, dated 1250–2', article in *Journal of the British Archaeological Association,* XIV, 1951.

Article on Chertsey kiln: see GARDNER below.

EMDEN, A. B. 'The Mediaeval tile pavement in the retro-choir', article in *Winchester Cathedral Record,* XVII, 1948.

FURNIVAL, W. J. *Leadless Decorative Tiles, Faience and Mosaic,* (published at Stone, Staffordshire), 1904.

GARDNER, J. S., and EAMES, ELIZABETH. 'A Tile kiln at Chertsey Abbey', article in *Journal of the British Archaeological Association,* XVII, 1954.

GILYARD-BEER, R. *Cleeve Abbey, Somerset,* Department of the Environment guidebook, (1962 reprint).

HABERLY, LOYD. *English Mediaeval Paving-tiles,* (Oxford), 1937. (Illustrated, and had full bibliography to date, but deals only with Oxford region.)

HOBSON, R. L. *Catalogue of the Collection of English Pottery in the British Museum,* (British Museum), 1903.

HOHLER, CHRISTOPHER. 'Mediaeval Pavingtiles in Buckinghamshire', article in *Records of the Buckinghamshire Archaeological Society,* XIV, 1941/2.

HOLLAND-MARTIN, R. 'Mediaeval heraldic and other tile pavements in Worcestershire', article, mainly on the Bredon Church tiles, in *Transactions of the Worcester Archaeological Society,* new series, 10, 1933.

HOLLIDAY, J. R. 'Hales Owen Abbey' (on Chertsey-type tiles excavated in late nineteenth century and majority then re-covered with soil), article in *The Birmingham and Midland Institute Archaeological Society transactions*, 1871.

HUGGINS, RHONA. 'Floor Tiles', Appendix 2 to report on excavations at Waltham Abbey, published in *Transactions of the Essex Archaeological Society*, 3rd. series, vol. II, part 3, 1970.

JAMES, M. R. 'Rare Mediaeval Tiles and their Story', article on tiles from Tring (showing the 'Apocryphal Infancy of Christ') in *The Burlington Magazine*, XLIII, 1922.

JEWITT, LLEWELLYN. *Ceramic Art of Great Britain,* (London) 2 volumes, 1878.
'On a Tile-kiln and Some Paving and Other Tiles Recently Discovered at Repton, Derbyshire', article in *The Reliquary*, VIII, 1868.

KEEN, LAURENCE. 'A Series of Seventeenth- and Eighteenth-Century Lead-glazed Relief Tiles from North Devon', article in *Journal of the British Archaeological Association*, XXXII, 1969.

KNAPP, G. E. C. 'The Mediaeval Tiles of Winchester Cathedral', article in *Winchester Cathedral Record*, 25, 1956.

LANE, ARTHUR. *A Guide to the Collection of Tiles*, Victoria and Albert Museum, 1939, (still available).

LETHABY, W. R. 'The romance tiles of Chertsey Abbey', article in *The Walpole Society Annual II*, 1913.
Westminster Abbey Re-examined, 1925.

LOOMIS, R. S. *Illustrations of mediaeval romance on tiles from Chertsey Abbey*, University of Illinois off-print, 1916.

MARTIN, GRAHAM. *Chiltern Churches*, 1972.

MAYES, P. 'A Mediaeval Tile Kiln at Boston, Lincolnshire', article in *Journal of the British Archaeological Association*, 28, 1965.

MYRES, J. N. L. 'Butley Priory, Suffolk', (section 5: 'The Finds'), article in *Archaeological Journal*, XC, 1933.

NICHOLS, JOHN GOUGH. *Examples of Decorative Tiles, sometimes called encaustic,* 1845.

NOPPEN, J. G. *The Chapter House, Westminster Abbey*, revised by S. E. Rigold, Department of the Environment guidebook, (sixth impression) 1970.

NOTT, JAMES. *Malvern Priory Church*, published in Great Malvern, Worcestershire, not dated – but about 1895.

PICCOLPASSO, CIPRIANO. *The Three Books of the Potter's Art* (mid-C 16 Italian treatises), translated and edited by Bernard Rackham and Alfred Van de Put, published by the Victorian and Albert Museum, 1934.

RACKHAM, BERNARD. *Mediaeval English Pottery*, 1948, (& revised edition published by Faber & Faber, 1972).

RENAUD, FRANK. 'The Uses and Teachings of Ancient Encaustic Tiles', article in *Transactions of the Lancashire and Cheshire Antiquarian Society* (Manchester), IX, 1892.

RICHARDSON, JAMES S. 'A Thirteenth-Century Tile Kiln at North Berwick, East Lothian, and Scottish Medieval Ornamental Floor Tiles', article in *Proceedings of the Society of Antiquaries of Scotland*, LXIII, 1928–9.

SALZMAN, L. F. *Building in England Down to* 1540: *a documentary history*, 1952 (section on tiles).

SHAW, HENRY. *Specimens of Tile Pavements*, London, 1858.

SHURLOCK, MANWARING. *Tiles from Chertsey Abbey, Surrey*, editions published in 1885 and 1913.

SLADE, C. F. 'Paving Tiles of Reading Abbey', article in *Berkshire Archaeological Journal*, 64, 1969.

STEVENS, FRANK. 'The Inlaid Paving Tiles of Wiltshire', article in *Wiltshire Archaeological Magazine*, XLVII, 1935–37.

STOUGHTON, F. T. S. *Worcestershire* (Little Guide), 1922, (section of introduction and text entries on tiles).

VIDLER, LEOPOLD A. 'Floor Tiles and Kilns near the site of St. Bartholomew's Hospital, Rye', article in *Sussex Archaeological Collections*, LXXII, (1932), with further articles in vols. LXXIV (1933) & LXXVII (1936).

WARD, JOHN. 'Notes on the Mediaeval Pavement and Wall Tiles of Derbyshire', article in *Derbyshire Archaeological and Natural History Society Journal*, 14, 1892.
(Despite the title the text has no mention of wall tiles.)

WARD-PERKINS, J. B. 'English Medieval Embossed Tiles', article in *Archaeological Journal*, XCIV, 1937.
'A Late Thirteenth-Century Tile-Pavement at Cleeve Abbey', article in *Proceedings of the Somerset Archaeological and Natural History Society*, LXXXVII, 1941.
Sections on tiles in the *Medieval Catalogue* published by the London Museum, 1954.

173

With WILLIAMS-HUNT, P. D. R. 'The Medieval Floor Tiles at St. Mary's Priory, Hurley, Berks', article in *Berkshire Archaeological Journal*, XLII, 1938.

WHITCOMB, NORMA R. *The Mediaeval Floor Tiles of Leicestershire,* off-print of article published by the Leicestershire Archaeological and Historical Society, (Leicester), 1956.

WOOD, MARGARET. *The English Mediaeval House,* 1965.

Index

Numbers in italic refer to illustrations. Page numbers in italic refer to pages on which relevant unnumbered illustrations appear.

178